PERSONALIZED RANKING FOR SEARCH ENGINES BASED ON WEB USAGE ANALYSIS

by

Mohammad Suaib

PERSONALIZED RANKING FOR SEARCH ENGINES BASED ON WEB USAGE ANALYSIS

by

Mohammad Suaib

TABLE OF CONTENT

Title	Page No.
Cover Page	i
Certificate	ii
Declaration	iii
Copyright Transfer Certificate	iv
Acknowledgement	v
Table of Contents	vii
List of Tables	x
List of Figures	xi
List of Symbols & Abbreviations	xii
Abstract	xiv

		Title	Page No.
Chapter 1		**Introduction**	**1-17**
1.1		Introduction	1
1.2		Problem Description	2
1.3		Motivation	4
1.4		Objectives of the work	9
1.5		Research Methodology	11
1.6		Relevance of the work	12
1.7		Organization of thesis report	14
1.8		Conclusion	15
Chapter 2		**Literature Survey**	**18-41**
2.1		Background Study	18
	2.1.1	Web Structure Mining	19
	2.1.2	Web Content Mining	23
	2.1.3	Web Usage Mining	24
2.2		Study of related work	26
	2.2.1	Approaches to deal with web page ranking	26

		2.2.2	Approaches to deal with personalized web page ranking	30
		2.2.3	State of the art in personalized web page ranking	34
2.3		Conclusion		40
Chapter 3		**Study of Associative Classification**		**42-55**
3.1		Associative Classification		43
3.2		Associative Classification Process		45
3.3		Association Rule Mining Algorithm		47
		3.3.1	Apriori Algorithm	47
		3.3.2	Frequent Pattern growth algorithm	48
		3.3.3.	Greedy method	49
		3.3.4	Confidence Rules	49
3.4		Problems with Associative Classification		50
3.5		Associative Classification Schemes		50
		3.5.1	Classification Based on Association (CBA)	51
		3.5.2	Classification Based on Multiple Association Rules (CMAR)	52
		3.5.3	Classification Based on Predictive Association Rules (CPAR)	53
3.6		Steps in Associative Classification		53
3.7		Evaluation Techniques		53
3.8		Conclusion		55
Chapter 4		**Study of BAT Algorithm**		**56-67**
4.1		Nature inspired optimization Techniques		56
4.2		Virtual BAT algorithm		63
		4.2.1	Encoding & Fitness functions	64
		4.2.2	Frequency & Velocity	65
		4.2.3	Finding Global best (optimized position)	65
4.3		Conclusion		67

Chapter 5	**Proposed Approach**	**68-78**
5.1	Proposed System	68
5.2	Data Set description	69
5.3	Data Preprocessing	70
5.4	User Grouping	72
5.5	Pattern Analysis	73
5.6	Rule optimization	74
5.7	Conclusion	78
Chapter 6	**Result and Discussion**	**79-89**
6.1	Evaluation Parameters	79
6.2	Experimental Results	80
	6.2.1 Results	80
Chapter 7	**Conclusion and Future Work**	**90-93**
7.1	Conclusion	90
7.2	Future Work	92
References		**94-116**
List of Publications		**117**
Recommendation		**118-121**

LIST OF TABLES

Table No.	Particulars	Page No.
2.1	Comparative calculation of Page Ranking approaches	29
2.2	Query-Term Preference List Keyword Indexing	30
2.3	Various techniques for web user personalization	35-37
2.4	Comparative analysis among Page ranking approaches used in researches	38-39
5.1	Sample session details	72
5.2	User groups	73
6.1	Result of the proposed approach with varying number of iterations for D1 & D2	80
6.2	Result of the proposed approach with varying number of iterations for D2	81
6.3	Comparison of mined rules without optimization & with optimization	87
6.4	Comparison of proposed method with others	88

LIST OF FIGURES

Figure No.	Particulars	Page No.
2.1	Web Mining Category	18
4.1	Classification of Nature inspired Optimization Techniques	56
4.2	Flow diagram of PSO Algorithm	60
4.3	Flow chart of ACO algorithm	61
4.4	Flow chart of virtual BAT motion implementation	66
5.1	Block diagram of the proposed system	69
5.2	Flow chart for implementing virtual BAT motion	76
6.1	Precision & Accuracy of proposed system on D2 dataset	82
6.2	TPR value for datasets	82
6.3	Precision value for datasets	83
6.4	Recall value for datasets	84
6.5	F-measure value for datasets	85
6.6	Accuracy value for datasets	86
6.7	Result of rule optimization on D1	87
6.8	comparison of proposed method with ref. (Al-Asdi & Obaid, 2016)	88
6.9	comparison of proposed method with ref. (Malhotra & Rishi, 2018)	89

LIST OF ABBREVIATIONS

HITS	Hyper Link Induced Topic Search
PR	Page Rank
WPR	Weighted Page Rank
UIS	User Interest Score
TF-IDF	Term Frequency - Inverse Document Frequency
PWS	Personalized Web Search
CF	Collaborative filtering
DT	Decision Tree
NN	Neural Network
CAR	Class Association Rules
AC	Associative Classification
CBA	Classification Based on Associations
RG	Rule Generator
CMAR	Classification based on Multiple Association Rules
FP	Frequent Pattern
DIC	Dynamic Itemset Counting
CAR	Class Association Rules
CPAR	Classification Based on Predictive Association Rules
PSO	Particle Swarm Optimization
ACO	Ant Colony Optimization
CSA	Cuckoo Search Algorithm

TPR   True Positive Rate

FPR   False Positive Rate

1.1 Introduction

The introduction of high-speed internet and the rise in smart phone internet users has resulted in an unfathomable surge of internet data on the Web. Because there is no centralized monitoring of data to be kept, indexed, and retrieved on the web, Search Engines are faced with a difficult task of retrieving searched information from the Web not only in a timely manner, but also to the exact and near accuracy of user interest and intent. As a result of the exponential growth in the number of digital data on the web, Web Search Engines must be clever and capable of obtaining the requested information based on the needs and preferences of internet users. For this purpose, ranking web pages becomes an important task for the fact that it helps users in finding highly rated web-pages that are believed to be the most relevant to their intended search. But this task is not a simple task as it requires to infer and figure out the interest and intent of the user making search thereon web. To apprehend the user's interest in order to rank the web-pages several metrics have been proposed by the researchers wherein ranking directly corresponds to the quality and relevance of web-pages explored during the search (Micarelli et al., 2007). Taking this objective forward, a search engine needs to be developed which can take up the user's queries in the most understanding manner and then successfully optimize the ranking of online webpages according to the user's requirements using web usage data (Bao et al., 2007).

Research statistics reveals that, in most of the cases the search engine queries are quite brief & unspecified, and users might have totally different set of intents for exactly the same query during the search. To simplify this statement let's think about a scenario wherein a real estate agent uses the keyword "office" in order to find a piece of land area available for office space, while an IT acquainted person or professional might use exact same keywords in query to find popular Microsoft Word-Processing software MS-office. Hence the search strings are susceptible to the ambiguity when being evaluated from user's perspective and leads to produce trivial end results by search engines. To address these disparities across users, customized search, which tailors search results depending on a user's interests, has seen a recent rise of interest. Personalized search has the potential to greatly enhance user experience, given the vast and rising significance of search engines (Metzger & Flanagin, 2013; Qiu & Cho, 2006).

To our utter surprise, researchers have revealed the fact that the great majority of users are hesitant to offer clear feedback on search results and their personal likings. They usually stay refrained of opining on end result of their web-search for the fear of being read of their psychological behavior. As a result, a tailored search engine aimed at a huge audience must have to automatically learn the user's preferences without getting any explicit feedback-input from the user's side (K. Liu, 2018).

1.2 Problem Description

We've seen an enormous surge in the volume of digital data and internet users in the last year. The vast raw data must be obtained sensibly and efficiently as the size of internet-based information expands dramatically (K. Liu, 2018). There are numerous methods and techniques for obtaining, tailoring, and using digital data to meet our needs. It's becoming more difficult for search engines to figure out what a web visitor is looking for. The most primary work of Search Engines is to retrieve the most relevant and concrete information on the web with respect to the searched phrases or keywords typed by user(s) which satisfies the user's query (Kasneci et al., 2008; Kobayashi & Takeda, 2000).

Comprehending the user's intent behind his or her query is really very challenging. Understanding the underlying intent of the user's query is extremely crucial for a search engine to provide the most precise search results befitting and matching the user's complete satisfaction and requirements (Palotti et al., 2016). Despite the fact that there are several online search technologies, many grounds and situations exist in which search engine users are dissatisfied with the search results generated by them. Users, for the same query, may possess entirely different preferences and intents for the same Web search. Likewise, different query-requests, from the same user but from a distinct region, may mean different in perspective and end results. A query may take on multiple intents and meanings depending on the intended circumstances, which can only be fully understood by the user (Chapelle et al., 2011; Sakai & Song, 2011).

To visualise and understand the underlying problem of web search we may hold following discussion and scenario wherein the web users strive for obtaining the most promising search results sufficing their need and search interest (Zhou, 2013).

Case-1: Consider a query that only has the word "Paint" in it. This term may now cause confusion for the search engine when understanding the true meaning of the word during the search. It might be used to get different shades of color variations for painting a home wall, or it could be used to refer to a Microsoft Paint (MS Paint) utility software for coloring or sketching on a computer.

Case-2: A user query having just a keyword "**silver**" for web-search. Now this keyword may be interpreted in many ways with following possible intents of the user-

a) He / She might be searching for an ornament made of silver,

b) He / She might be searching for a color to paint a wall or something alike

c) Or they even may be looking for a kind of fish found in specific part of the world.

Outlining the problem as described above, we need to come up with personalized web search engine to mitigate such cases of the search because traditional search engines used to provide only alike set of results without apprehending the intent of user behind the query. This can be achieved through ranking web pages based on web-usage analysis (Valsamidis et al., 2011; Yan & Gerstein, 2011). A Web usage analysis is based on the user's previous usage history and can assist to enhance the ranking of web sites according to the user's requirements (Cheung & Vogel, 2013; J. Lu et al., 2015). It aims at providing an effective service mechanism for tailored search engine page ranking based on online web-usage statistics of users with respect to several qualitative metrics (Bozdag, 2013; Tintarev & Masthoff, 2015).

1.3 Motivation

The internet has become an integral component of our daily life. It has led billions of individuals all around the world to participate and collaborate in accessing and sharing information across the world. It is possible only internet that people today can access practically any type of information at any time, from anywhere by just making a search on their internet-devices (such as smartphones, tablets Laptop etc.). They are just a click away from any information which is globally available around them on internet. "Searching is an Art" to make it true "Search Engines" come in a big picture. Search engine plays a vital role particularly exploring information within large and voluminous websites such as E-commerce websites, corporate sites, and social networking sites etc (Jang et al., 2015).

The motivation behind this research may better be described by holding following discussions and observing factual records with respect to internet usage across the globe.

- As now till 2021, 4.66 billion (60% of global population) active internet users are there across the world. Every month, approximately 744 million users used their smartphone for surfing the internet, digging out email, browsing social networks, performing online transactions, and getting into numerous web activities alongside. People are increasingly surfing the internet while on the go. For example, one could wish to know more about a neighborhood restaurant or a new destination they are going to visit (Ghose et al., 2013; Osman et al., 2012).

- Although the capabilities of online search engines have gone improved so far and are gradually improvising, nevertheless there are still a number of issues that need to be solved to make search engines even better and more efficient. For instance, the issue of irrelevant search results is one big barrier. Short, unclear and inexplicit searches or semantic inconsistencies are the most common causes of irrelevant search results (Glanville, 2019; Hofmeister et al., 2017). To quote a few of such cases are: "Apple", "Pascal", "Match", "Conductor" etc. based on the context and intent of the user, all of these keywords might have completely different interpretations and meanings (Fernández et al., 2011; Stuckey et al., 2013).

- The other major cause for the aforementioned problem can be labeled as, "One-size-fits-all" strategy adopted by almost all contemporary search engines being used till date, wherein a same set of results is returned for all users when they submit the same query in various different situations. Search engines provide a list of search results depending upon the user's query but in reality these search engines disregard the user's personal interests, context of their quest of search, and individualist information requirements (Buttcher et al., 2016; Shokouhi, 2013). Consequently, a user at times has to navigate through a lot of vain pages containing useless information before discovering what they're actually looking for (Birnhack, 2011; Rheingold, 2012).

- Web service companies may employ personalized web search to meet their customers' needs & expectations and thereby can succeed in creating a unique user experience. Personalization has been researched and implemented in the field of Human Computer Interaction, Information System, Computer Science and Business Marketing as well. Various personalization techniques have been implemented to provide special treatment to the users and to gain users attention with the expectation of high return in business (Ricci et al., 2011; Sunikka & Bragge, 2012). Personalized search not only helps users in hitting the right corner with least effort and time to suffice his/her need of information but also, indirectly, helps web-service providers (like E-Commerce) to bring the most promising customer to its doorstep (Gao et al., 2010; Rong & Liu, 2010).

- The task of apprehending users' interest and complying it with that of the worldwide information stored on the internet is also extremely complex and it attracts large-scale novel research endeavors from industry-academia personnel and from business-world as well.

- To fill a vacuum in existing research into diverse personalization design features applicable in web search engines, and the various roles they play in users' decision-making, and to answer the growing demand for meaningful assistance in web personalization.

The above-mentioned points have served as a factor of motivation to me to begin with the research in the domain of web personalization search engine to contribute to the noble cause of improvising search engine efficiency and accuracy for internet users across the world.

1.3.1 A Brief Summary of Previous Research

Personalization research may be roughly classified into three streams, according to previous research patterns (Desai, 2019). The first looks at process-oriented characteristics of personalization techniques using various methodologies and algorithms. For instance, personalization that is adaptive and adaptable, data mining tools, cookies, and push techniques are just a few examples of that case (Romero & Ventura, 2013).

The second section looks at user-centered customization, such as user duties, privacy concerns, and app context. The third envisages into how tailored personalized webpages are presented to users and how successful they are (Toch et al., 2012) (R. L. Kumar et al., 2004) Personalization has been defined in the third stream as the process of altering a system's functionality, interface, content quality, or uniqueness in order to maximize its individualistic pertinence to that person (Blom & Monk, 2003; Fan & Poole, 2006). The knob-twisting of those components of a website that are shown to a user that meet the user's wants is referred to as "serving the purpose in its true sense"(Wu et al., 2003).

This research focuses on the design component of personalization utilized in business and social-media platforms (Networking), as well as the impact it has on users' decisions to revisit or return to these sites (Moe & Fader, 2004; Park, 2014).

1.3.2 Gap in Existing Research

Research in area of computer science and it focuses on different techniques and algorithm to implement personalization and also measures the evaluation performance of web personalization like recommendation systems, with accuracy metrics (e.g., mean, precision, rank, absolute error and recall). Researches in Information System design broadly focus on behavioral and cognitive aspect of personalization with optimum design, implementation and its affective reaction on user's decision making (Häubl & Trifts, 2000). Fan and Poole studied personalization aspects with respect to Information system design, Tam and Ho looked at the effects of personalizing on user processing of information and decision-making(Fan & Poole, 2006; Ho et al., 2007). Personalization's perceived usefulness and simplicity of use, on the other hand, is a key component in recruiting new users. In the context of the technology acceptance theory, researchers (Komiak & Benbasat, 2006) investigate the impact of perceived personalization and familiarity on emotional and cognitive trust (Venkatesh et al., 2010). More research topics for studying online personalization in the context of management science were offered by Murthi and Sarkar (Murthi & Sarkar, 2003). They pointed out that one of the most commonly asked questions by Web personalization practitioners is: "Which items should be offered to influence individual customers' consideration sets?" (Murthi & Sarkar, 2003).

(M. Wang & Yen, 2010) looks into how a Web personalization technique affects the formation of users' consideration sets and their final decision outcomes. The fundamental subject of How to design personalization in the context of client retention was investigated by Kwon, and Kim (Kwon & Kim, 2012). Recently research has gained increasing attention on interactive way of Human Computer Interaction. Effective personalized website design is a critical topic that must be investigated in order to satisfy the expectations and changing needs of users(Ping Zhang, 2001; Verdegem & Verleye, 2009).

Varying parts of personalized design have different effects on user perception and meet different types of user needs. However, studies in the past have focused predominantly on simply one or more components of personalization, e.g. content personalization (Blom & Monk, 2003; De Oliveira et al., 2013; Fredrikson & Livshits, 2011; Komiak & Benbasat, 2006; Kwon & Kim, 2012; Lavie et al., 2010) but the usefulness of online personalization in search engines has received minimal research (Dabholkar & Sheng, 2012; Komiak & Benbasat, 2006; Liang et al., 2006; Venkatesh et al., 2010). Only a few studies have looked into the roles that multiple dimensions of personalization play. In fact, there is a serious lack of actionable guidance on personalization design issues and effective personalized web design in the existing literature(M. Wang & Yen, 2010). To fill these research gaps, this study conducts a thorough assessment of the literature on customization, provides a methodologically designed framework for personalized website design, and tests the impact of various components of personalization. Based on environmental psychology theory and TAM. This research looks into the various roles played by personalization dimensions, such as information personalization, presentation personalization, and navigation personalization (Sundar & Marathe, 2010; T.-C. Yang et al., 2013). From the fields of information systems and human-computer interaction, this study examines the multidisciplinary nature of personalized website design and its impact on users' intentions to return to the site(Gómez et al., 2014; Thongpapanl & Ashraf, 2011).

1.4 Objectives of the Work

The objective of this research can be apprehended and contemplated by going through the research questions which are yet to be answered in a better and concrete way-

1.4.1 Research Questions

The subsequent research questions will be addressed by this study:

- What popular web-search personalization schemes have been devised and implemented in various popular search engines and what has been its effect?
- How various web-personalization aspects impact on end result of web-search and affect user's' satisfaction with utilitarian and affective reaction?

- How a personalized web-search can be improvised using optimization techniques that influences the users to stay quenched to their utter satisfaction?

1.4.2 Research Objectives

Our current research focusses to identify the important design views of web personalization and to examine the roles portrayed by these aspects. This research is primarily based on exploring a way and means to develop a service mechanism for personalized search engine which produces the most promising search results to the user in accordance with the need, interest, mean and intent of user. Hence the primary goal of this research is to develop an effective approach for search engine tailored web page ranking based on web-use information. To achieve this objective, a range of widely used and most accepted optimization algorithms are to be explored and studied which can be exploited and tailored for the purpose of achieving expected outcome in a personalized web-search. The rule-based optimization algorithms used in providing optimized solution (here is search result)-in particular the nature inspired algorithms(Zang et al., 2010) like **BAT algorithm** (X.-S. Yang & He, 2013), **ACO**(Albinati et al., 2015), **ABC** & **Apriory Algorithms** (Ferrini & Scarpa, 2007) and conceptual theory of heuristics (Daly et al., 2012; Gigerenzer & Gaissmaier, 2011), system learning approaches such as-Artificial Intelligence (Bhardwaj et al., 2018; Taulli & Oni, 2019), Deep learning and Neural Network (Goldberg, 2017; Kamath et al., 2019) etc are some of the primary research outcomes to be included in my research study which can help in achieving the intended solution for designing personalized web search engine. The goal of the study is to look at several areas of personalization design that have an influence on a user's mental and pragmatic experience (Perceived intent of Use, Perceived Usefulness, Satisfaction), as well as the capacity to improve user contentment with personalized online search (J. Liu et al., 2010; Lops et al., 2011).

This study takes a user-centered approach, attempting to explain and forecast how consumers would react to a customized online information search engine. A better knowledge of the psychological and behavioral motivations of users, as well as their behaviour, attitude, and aim, will help in developing a way better personalized web search engine.

1.5 Research Methodology

The research methodology can be better described by mentioning our research design used in this work.

1.5.1 Research Design

Research Design is a design for collecting data depending on the nature of the research, which might be qualitative or quantitative, exploratory or descriptive.

This is a descriptive study with a qualitative focus, as we look into the impact of personalization on web users' behavioral intentions and satisfaction.

There are three types of research design: (1) exploratory research design, (2) descriptive and diagnostic research design, and (3) hypothesis testing research design. (Kothari, 2017; Nunan et al., 2020).

Formularize research studies are another name for exploratory research projects. The primary goal of these investigations is to formulate an issue for further inquiry or to develop workable hypotheses from an operational standpoint(Bell et al., 2010). The development of new ideas and insights is a primary focus in such studies and design thinking process (Dorst, 2011). How can user interest score be calculated and better web-page ranking can be achieved for a personalized web-search. As a result, the research design appropriate for such investigations must be flexible enough to allow for consideration of many facets of the subject under investigation. Because the research problem, which was first described broadly, is transformed into one with a more definite meaning in exploratory research, inbuilt adaptability in research design is required. This may entail adjustments in the research technique for acquiring relevant data (Gaikwad, 2017; Litman et al., 2017).

Research can also be categorized based on nature of the data: qualitative and quantitative. Quantitative research is based on determining the quantity or amount of something. It can be used to describe phenomena that have a numerical value (Bloomfield & Fisher, 2019). Qualitative research, on the other side, is involved with qualitative phenomena, such as those involving or linked to quality or kind like investigating reasons for human behavior (Grossoehme, 2014; Silverman, 2020). Combining these two qualitative and quantitative research helps in attaining phenomenal results research domains (Brannen, 2017; Östlund et al., 2011). Motivational Research which focuses at investigating the underlying aims and desires. In the behavioral sciences, where the goal is to identify the true motivations of human nature, qualitative research is very significant (Dörnyei & Ushioda, 2021; Koballa Jr & Glynn, 2013). We may evaluate the many elements that push people to behave in a certain way or make them like or detest a certain thing through such research. However, it should be noted that qualitative research must be used. (Hennink et al., 2020; Hesse-Biber & Leavy, 2010; Merriam & Tisdell, 2015)

1.6 Contribution and Relevance of the Work

This study significantly contributes in developing mechanism for page ranking in personalized web-search engine by identifying different personalization aspects like web personalization, navigation personalization and calculating user interest score based on web-usage history of user. The findings of the study are theoretically based on a large corpus of prior research on web personalization using a page ranking technique. This research contributes towards measuring important dimensions of personalization i.e. what to personalize and identifying various aspects of personalization used in personalized web searches which produces effective search results in conformity with user interest and intent. This research helps search engine to obtain, extract and locate the most appropriate search results (list of web links) which accurately satisfies user quest of web-information within least amount of time and effort.

This Research also throws light on how this personalization aspect impacts the users' satisfaction and their decision making of accepting the end-results returned by search engine with cognitive and hedonic influence on their searching experience. Though there have been sever researches on web personalization techniques conducted in the past but there is limited research in personalized web-page ranking for web search engines which provides the most optimized search results which achieve a higher degree of users' satisfaction and higher acceptance rate of result.

To address this gap in the previous researches in computer science and engineering, several rule optimization techniques were explored and some of them are selected to be exploited and then implemented within the proposed solution designed for personalized page ranking for search engines. In particular, we have investigated the roles of information personalization, user interest scoring, and navigation pattern recognition on enhancing the cognitive and affective determinants of user intention to rank and produce the most promising search results having the highest degree of acceptance by user within least trail.

On practical background this research of mine contributes towards information acquisition on internet in particular and in general it contributes on theoretical background to the field of

Computer Science Engineering and Information Technology, as well as other alike disciplines such as Artificial Intelligence (Ertel, 2018), Neural network (Hinton et al., 2015), Deep Learning (Goodfellow et al., 2016) and Nature Inspired Algorithms(Zang et al., 2010) (Fister Jr et al., 2013; X.-S. Yang, 2020).

1.7 Organization of Thesis Report

The entire research work has been organized on the following pattern-.

Chapter 2

This chapter presents a comprehensive literature review of the diverse range of Page ranking algorithms, approaches and methodologies that have been developed and used in the past for personalized web-searching. Many competing methodologies have been analyzed and selected to be used in the proposed solution considering its suitability and proven effectivity.

Chapter 3

This chapter discusses Approach and nature inspired algorithms (Zang et al., 2010) for optimization of solutions. The **Apriory Algorithm** has been discussed in this chapter for its novelty, effectivity, suitability and modality with respect to our proposed mechanism for personalized page ranking for search engine.

Chapter 4

This chapter holds discussion on the proposed solution which is a newly proposed techniques developed through exploiting BAT(X.-S. Yang, 2010) algorithm for optimizing the page ranking outcomes to locate and yield the most relevant and most promising search results from user's perspective.

Chapter 5

This chapter renders light upon the output results obtained from the implementation of proposed and developed techniques for personalized page ranking mechanism for search engine. It demonstrates the simulated results and performance analysis of proposed work in comparison to other existing techniques dealing in the field of personalized web-search.

Chapter 6

The conclusion, contribution, and scope of future study are all explored in this chapter. It highlights the study findings by emphasizing the research gap and issue description, as well as responding to research questions. It covers the complete research process, from presenting the notion of Page ranking to factors of customization, identifying the research gap, providing a solution, modelling and testing the suggested work, and verifying and proving the solution's innovation.

1.8 Conclusions

With an increase in internet user, there has been an abrupt and massive increase in volume of internet data. Billions and trillions of web page are scattered across the world of internet to store and sustain the unfathomable digital data. It throws an exceptional challenge to search engines to explore and locate the most relevant and most appropriate web page, out of these trillions of pages, in response to the query of an internet user making a web-search.

To make it easy for a search engine the concept of page ranking in the purview of user interest and his past preferences came in to existence. Page-Rank is a worldwide rating of all available web pages based only on their position in the Web graph structure, independent of content. The ranking of web pages obtained by the search engine is highly important in order to provide the most promising and most effective response to the online user making web search (query).

Using PageRank, one may sort search results so that the most essential and relevant Web pages appear first in the results. PageRank may be used to sort a small number of commonly used pages that can answer the majority of user-generated queries. Based on the user's online activity, we may estimate his interests, which can be utilized to enhance the ranking of the web pages obtained.

Hence, it would be fair to say that PageRank might be an excellent technique to find highly relevant and representative pages to display in a cluster search results. In addition, the Web graph's structure is highly beneficial for a number of information retrieval applications when using a Page-Rank technique (G. Kumar et al., 2011; Singh & Kumar, 2009).

Various methods and criteria have been used to determine the rankings of web sites based on the quality of the page and the user's interest-score. Web usage analysis based on the user's previous usage history can assist to enhance the ranking of web sites according to the user's requirements. Personalization of web pages using web mining techniques involves two phases: offline and online. The goal of the offline phase is to use the history and web log data to model the user's travel pattern. After that, the model is utilized to forecast a user's navigation pattern and make suggestions based on that prediction. The ability of association mining to predict user browsing behaviour for online tailored recommendations has been utilized and demonstrated in this study.

In this research, webpage ranking is determined through a hybrid technique based on an optimized association rule mining. The implicit data is retrieved from the user's web usage log (stored in web server logs), and the designed solution is then implemented using the BAT algorithm. Along with the existing state-of-the-art methodologies for web page personalization, a thorough comparison study and validation is performed. The findings obtained so far have demonstrated a spectacular performance in terms of achieving the desired result with higher degree of user acceptance and search accuracy. Finally, in terms of web page personalization, our presented approach beats the competing schemes and delivers remarkable benchmark performance.

2.1 Background Study

The Internet is a global network that is continually changing and an abode of mammoth unstructured web-data (Grace et al., 2011). The Internet is the largest data source on the planet. The technique of gathering and mining useful data from the internet is known as web mining. Data mining, ML, NLP, information retrieval, multimedia, statistics, databases, and other disciplines are all part of this multidisciplinary field. The amount of knowledge available on the Internet is enormous and readily accessible. Knowledge is derived not only from web page contents, but also from the Web's distinguishing feature, its hyperlink construction, and the variety of its contents (G. Kumar et al., 2011). The examination of these qualities frequently provides fresh knowledge and fascinating trends that might help users increase their productivity; thus, approaches for extracting data from the web are an intriguing research topic. These methodologies aid in the extracting knowledge from Web data, with structural or utilization (Web log) data being employed in the mining process at least once (Grace et al., 2011). In this chapter, we first present an overview of Web mining principles and tools, before delving deeper into Web structure mining.

Web mining duties are often divided into three categories: content mining, structure mining, and use mining. All three areas are concerned with the process of obtaining implicit, previously unknown, and useful knowledge gleaned through the web. Each one is dedicated to a specific form of Web mining object. The Web categories and their items are depicted in Figure 2.1.

We'll give you a quick overview of each of the categories in the sections below.

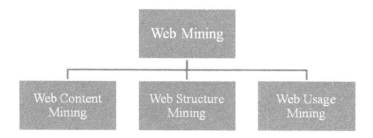

Figure 2.1 Web Mining Category

2.1.1 Web Structure Mining

Only the text on pages is used by web information retrieval technologies, which ignores crucial information in links. Web structure mining is used to create a structural overview of websites and pages. As a result, structure mining focuses on link information, which constitutes a significant portion of web data. Interesting and enlightening information about their connectedness in the web subset may be uncovered given a group of interconnected web articles (Tyagi & Gupta, 2018). From the web tuples in the web tables, we wish to extract the following structural information. In a web table, we calculate the frequency of local connections in web tuples. Different web documents on the same server are connected together via local links. This information is provided on web tuples (linked documents) in the web table, which provide additional information about interrelated documents on the same server. This also measure the webpage completeness by ensuring that the majority of closely related material is accessible from the same location. Local links connecting "route information with air-fares and timetables" will be more prevalent on an airline's home page than external links, for example.

It's worth noting that our web warehouse is filled utilizing a user-initiated query graph. If the returned results (i.e., web tuples) include a higher number of local links, we can deduce that the query is crawling some specific web sites locally. In this situation, one can optimize the query graph for the next execution of such a query so that crawling with those sites can begin immediately. When a web crawler traverses through many unbound nodes and links, but only finds actual web pages at a single site, this situation may occur.

It's worth noting that the information you're looking for can be spread over multiple servers on the network. Local links show that integrated content is also available at a specific web site, albeit in other files. As a result, such data can shorten the time it takes for a query to be executed over the internet.

We can measure the occurrence of web tuples in a web table with interior links (links that are within the same document). This statistic assesses an online document's capacity to refer to other relevant web pages included inside the same document. Web document flow is also measured. Other local news topics, for example, should always be mentioned in a newspaper (within the same news-paper).

This means that all of the required data is contained inside the same file. Counting all the web tuples in its database with global links (links that cross many web sites). This metric evaluates the prominence of web papers as well as the ability to link similar or related materials across multiple websites. For example, study documents pertaining to "semi structured data" will be made available on a variety of websites, and these sites should be visible to other connected sites by using popular terms like "additional relevant links" to provide cross references. A research article, for example, should include more external links since it should relate to other works in the subject. This reflects a research study's capacity to cross-reference other similar studies. The number of times identical web tuples appear in a web table or between web tables is counted.

This metric tracks online document replication across the web warehouse and can be used to identify mirrored sites, for example. According to this data, certain web pages offer comprehensive information on a variety of themes. We've also used duplicate web tuples to find out what's viewable on the web, for example. In the next section, we'll go through this topic. On average, it is worth to observe as how many web-rows are responded back to a query having keywords, for example, "Earth Science" versus searches with keywords such as "Bio Science" (Madria et al., 1999).

This can provide a rough estimate of the results returned in response to a number of common queries. This also indicates whether the results of such a query should be stored in our warehouse for future use. Another fascinating topic is determining the characteristic of the hierarchy or hyperlink network on a specific domain's web sites. When it comes educational sector URLs like.edu, for example, one might be interested in learning how most educational school websites are designed in terms of information flow. What is the flow of the data they offer, and how do they link conceptually? Is it imaginable to extract abstract hierarchical information in order to create specific domain web sites? This may aid in the generalization of information flow in web pages that represent data in a certain domain (Laender et al., 2002). This will aid in the development of a standard web schema or educational institute wrappers, for example. As a result, query processing could be simplified. What is each node's (web document) and out-degree? What do in- and out-degrees mean? A high in-degree, for example, could indicate that a web site or publication is quite popular. A high out-degree, on the other hand, could indicate a bright website. The connection of a facility is also measured by Out-degree. In the following part, we'll go over these concerns. We'd like to learn about the relationships between web pages if one is directly linked to another or if they're in close proximity to one another. The following types of relationships could exist. Both web pages may be related by synonyms or ontologies, or they may have similar subjects, and both web pages may be authored by the same person if they are located on the same server(Madria et al., 1999).

While the above information is obtained at the inter-document level, web structure mining can also be used to determine the structure of individual online documents. Web document structure mining can be used to discover the structure (schema) of web pages. While this is handy for navigating, it may also be used to perform other tasks such as comparing and merging web page layouts. Structure mining like this would make it easier to categorize and cluster web documents based on their structure. By providing a reference schema, it will also assist in the introduction of database approaches for accessing information in web pages (R. Cooley et al., 1997; Stumme et al., 2006). Semantic markup's accessibility. We'll go over a few of the link mining jobs that can be used to Web structure mining in the following sections.

1. Link-based Classification. The most recent upgrading of a traditional data mining activity to linked domains is link-based classification (R. Cooley et al., 1997). The goal is to predict the category of a web page based on the words on the page, connections between pages, anchor text, html tags, and other web page attributes.

2. Link-based Cluster Analysis. Cluster analysis is used to identify naturally occurring sub-classes. The data is organized into categories, with like things grouped together and different objects segregated into distinct groups. Link-based cluster analysis, unlike the prior job, is unsupervised and may be used to find hidden patterns in data (Chopra & Ataullah, 2013; Getoor, 2003).

3. The Type of Link Predicting the existence of links involves a wide range of tasks, such as predicting the type of link between two entities or predicting the purpose of a link.

4. Link Stability. Weights could be associated with links.

5. Connect Cardinality. Predicting the number of links between objects is the main task here.

2.1.2 Web Content Mining

Web content mining is the process of examining the contents of web data. What does it mean to "mine material from the web?" is an open question. Because we might anticipate to extract similar sorts of information from unstructured data existing in web publications, web content mining is effectively analogous to data mining approaches for relational databases. Because of the unstructured nature of web data, web content mining requires a specialised technique. The web contains a variety of data types, including textual data, image data, audio and video, and so on. At the moment, WHOWEDA's primary focus is on extracting relevant information from web hypertext data. We focus on the following web content mining challenges in the context of web warehouses:

The similarities and differences between web content mining and traditional datamining in the context of web warehousing. A relational database's data is flat and well-organized in a tabular format defined by attributes with specified domains. In web data, documents are completely unstructured, and distinct attributes in documents may have semantically comparable meaning across the WWW or vice versa. For example, one website may display the price of the same car as a numeric figure, whereas another may display it in words. An attribute may have an atomic value in some documents, but a collection of values in others. To begin content mining, you must first solve the problem of semantic integration among web documents.

Web content mining is the process of extracting meaningful information from a webpage's content using text mining tools. A webpage can be a simple text document or a multimedia document with tables, forms, images, video, and audio. Web content mining is the process of extracting relevant information from web pages. Web content mining can be classified into two categories: agent-based and database-based approaches. The first method tries to improve information retrieval and filtering, and it falls into one of three types (Albanese A. 2004).

Intelligent Search Agents: These agents employ domain features and user profiles to find relevant information and then organize and analyze it.

Information Filtering/Categorization: These agents retrieve, filter, and categorize open hypertext Web documents using information retrieval techniques and features.

Personalized Web Agents: These agents learn user preferences and discover Web information based on these preferences as well as the preferences of other users who share similar interests.

2.1.3 Web Usage Mining

Web use mining is the automated identification and analysis of patterns in click streams and associated data collected or generated as a result of user interactions with Web resources on one or more Web sites (Evans & Mathur, 2018). The goal is to capture, model, and assess the patterns and characteristics of website visitors. The found patterns are often depicted as collections of places, objects, or services that are frequently utilized by groups of individuals that have similar requirements or interests. Like any other data mining approach, the complete Web use mining process may be separated into three interdependent steps: Data collection and pre-processing, pattern finding, and pattern analysis are all part of the process. The click stream data is cleaned and partitioned into a collection of user transactions that reflect each user's behaviour over several visits to the site during the pre-processing step. Other sources of information, such as site content or structure, as well as semantic domain knowledge from site ontologism, can be utilized to pre-process or augment user transaction data (such as product catalogues or concept hierarchies). Statistical, database, and machine learning procedures are used in the pattern discovery step to uncover hidden patterns that reflect typical user activity, as well as summary information on Web resources, sessions, and users (Zaiane, 2001; ZUBI & Riani, 2013). The found patterns and statistics are further evaluated and filtered in the last phase of the process, potentially resulting in aggregate user models that may be fed into applications such as recommendation engines, visualization tools, Web analytics, and report generation tools (Eirinaki & Vazirgiannis, 2003). The remainder of this chapter examines Web usage mining as a process, as well as the concepts and techniques that are commonly used in each of the steps listed above.

Web usage mining has evolved into an important tool for developing more customized, user-friendly, and business-friendly Web services. Adaptive information systems, customization services, Web analytics tools, and content management systems have already benefited from data pre-processing, modelling, and mining methodologies applied to Web data. The need for intelligent analysis of Web usage data will grow in tandem with the complexity of Web applications and user engagement with these apps. Web usage mining is effective at collecting item-to-item and user-to-user linkages and similarities at the user session level. Such patterns provide little insight into the underlying reasons for grouping such products or users together without the benefit of deeper domain expertise. Furthermore, the Web's inherent and increasing heterogeneity has necessitated Web-based applications to integrate a diverse range of data types from various channels and sources more effectively (Baker et al., 2002). As a result, concentrating on techniques and architectures for more effective integration and mining of content, usage, and Structured data from heterogeneous sources will almost probably result in the next generation of more helpful and smarter apps, as well as more sophisticated Web usage mining technologies capable of extracting insight from Web user interactions (R. W. Cooley, 2000; Psaromiligkos et al., 2011).

2.2 Study of related work

In this chapter we have discussed different page ranking algorithms. We have extracted pros and cons of these approaches. Further we have studied web personalization techniques and found the state of art and research gap.

2.2.1 Approaches to deal with web page ranking

The size of the internet is continuously expanding, and the number of searches it can handle has also increased dramatically. As the number of people who use the internet grows, so does the number of queries that are submitted to search engines. As a result, search engines must be able to efficiently handle these queries. As a result, web mining techniques are used to extract only relevant pages from the database and offer consumers with the information they need. Web page ranking methods and web mining techniques are used to arrange the documents in order of relevance, importance, and content score (R. W. Cooley, 2000; Psaromiligkos et al., 2011). Some of the ranking algorithms that can be proposed are Link analysis algorithms, Personalized web search ranking algorithms, and Page Segmentation algorithms.

Algorithm for Link Analysis: The link analysis algorithm is based on the link structure of the document. The quality of search engine results is frequently lower than what users expect, and this quality can be significantly improved by sorting pages based on specific criteria based on links between pages. A page with numerous references, for example, must have something to say. Algorithm for determining page rank: The page rank algorithm was proposed by SurgeyBrin and L.Page (R. Cooley et al., 1997). Google uses this algorithm to rank web sites. The PageRank algorithm is built on the concept of a web graph (Thakkar et al., 2010), with web pages acting as nodes and links acting as edges. The rank value of a page indicates its importance. A vote of support is represented by a link to a page. A page's PageRank is determined by the number of links it has. A page with a high PageRank that is connected to by many other pages with a high PageRank earns a high PageRank as well (Batra & Sharma, 2013; Thakkar et al., 2010). If there are no links to a web page, that page does not have any support. PageRank is a probability distribution that depicts the likelihood that a person clicking on random links will end up on a specific website. PageRank can be determined for any large collection of documents. A probability is a number between 0 and 1 that represents the likelihood of something happening.

The HITS Algorithm is a method for calculating the number of hits on a Jon Kleinberg made his debut. Hyperlink-Induced Topic Search (HITS) (Asano et al., 2007) is a link analysis technique that ranks Web pages (also known as hubs and authorities). The hubs functioned as big directories that were not authoritative in terms of the content they contained, but rather served as collections of a large catalogue of material that directed readers to other authoritative pages. To put it another way, a good hub was a page that linked to a lot of other pages, and a good authority was a page that was linked by a lot of different hubs. As a result, each page is given two scores: authority, which assesses the value of the website's content, and hub value, which estimates the value of its linkages to other pages. We adjust auth (p) to be: h(i) n i=1 as per the Authority Update Rule: p. Where n is the total number of pages linked to p, and I denote a single page linked to p. In other words, a page's Authority score is the sum of all the Hub scores of pages that link to it. Update Rule: p, we update hub (p) to: auth(i) n i=1 Where n is the total number of pages to which p connects, and I denote a specific page to which p connects. As a result, a page's Hub score is the sum of all of its connecting pages' Authority scores(Selvan et al., 2012).

Focused Rank is a link-based ranking system that is based on the concept of targeted web browsers (Liu, C. 2004). A targeted search focuses on the appeal of a specific topic. Focused search addresses the multidimensionality of web information as well as the relationship between pages with comparable content. There is a link between pages u and v if they have a hyperlink between them and share at least one common topic. For a group of documents S and a list of topics, we obtain a set of probabilities P (d, ti), where d S and ti, of the document d belonging to a specific subject ti. There is less thematic overlap between two texts when they share few themes. Furthermore, when two pages belong to the same topic, the likelihood of them being included in those topics P (d, ti) is minimal, and so the topical overlap remains low. The online search results are ranked on the basis of weighted URL ranking algorithm, feature retrieval is done form available hyperlinks, anchor words, and user-interested sites. Occurrence of token were the base for retrieving results from the search engines and weight has been decided, then reassignment of weights are based on the user's interested domain, and similar procedure is used to retire re-ordering of the results. Some client-side algorithms are designed for personalization purposes, taking into account user moods, usage patterns, and search trends. In proposed analysis part, we analyzed and compared various methods related to link analysis named as Page Rank (PR), Weighted Page Rank (WPR), & Hyperlink-Induced Topic Search (HITS) (Zhang et al., 2017).The relevance of the results is ranked according to the user's interest. The TF-IDF measure and the user interest score are both taken into account when rating a result (UIS). When comparing several ranking schemes, we found that the hybrid (TF-IDF + UIS) scheme reflects our findings well, as available in table 2.1.

Table 2.1 Comparison table for different Page Ranking approaches on calculation basis

Preferred terms	TF-IDF	UIS	PPR	Hybrid (US+ TF-IDF)
Web	E	_	F	E
Web usage mining	G	A	G	FG
Web structure mining	G	G	-	Good
Web content mining	G	N	F	G
Personalization	E	G	F	E
Pattern analysis	G	G	P	E
Usage History	_	G	F	G
A-Adequate, E-Excellent, F- fair, G-Good, N- Neutral, FG- Fairly Good				

Personalized page rank can be affected by numerous factors and customized based user's preferences. The weights of the UIS and TF-IDF are varied while computing the rank, depending on the Query type and user's preferences. This hybrid scheme is bit different form typical Web page ranking systems, it uses a distinct set of criteria for deciding keyword index and calculating rank, as indicated in table 2.2.

The Implementation of the hybrid page ranking scheme to implement page re-ranking has following procedure:

• The keywords are weighed on the basis of TF-IDF measure in the initial set of text, and the same procedure is opted for user preferred network of concepts

• UIS based network is tracked, and recommended feature's weights are computed

• Final Resultant is ranked on the basis of computed UIS and TF-IDF acquired values.

Table 2.2 Query-Term Preference List Keyword Indexing

	Traditional	Hybrid
1	Web	Personalization
2	Web Mining	Usage data
3	Web structure mining	Profile
4	Web content mining	User data
5	Internet	Access log
6	Data mining	Web usage mining
7	Web Usage History	Pattern analysis

2.2.2 Approaches to deal with personalized web page ranking

Personalized web search (PWS) is a type of search technology that produces better search results and results that are personalized to the needs of individual users. To determine the user's intention and aims behind the issued query, data provided by the user must be collected and examined (Lee et al., 2005). The personalization process can result in dynamically generated suggestions, the construction of pages tailored to the user's needs, and the highlighting of existing hyperlinks that are specifically desired by users. The majority of previous Web Personalization research has focused on Web Usage Mining (Albanese et al., 2004). Google's Personalized Search, for example, allows users to define their favorite Web page categories. Some Web search systems employ relevant comments to process user requests or analyze users to better serve them by registering their demographic information early. Because these approaches require users to engage in additional activities beyond searching to indicate their decision manually, approaches capable of implicitly identifying users' information demands should be developed. Because the need for tailored search is growing, more studies must be conducted in order to deliver useful information while taking into account the users' circumstances. Many writers have proposed various personalized web search approaches, which are illustrated in the following section.

The most advanced system, "WebPersonalizer," was given by Mobasher et al (Mobasher, 1999). It's a strong framework for extracting meaningful data from web log files for the aim of making suggestions based on surfing commonalities between current and previous users. Data mining techniques such as association rule mining, clustering, sequential pattern discovery, and classification are used to determine interesting usage patterns once the data has been collected and cleaned. For boosting retrieval effectiveness, Fang Liu et al. proposed tailored Web search (F. Liu et al., 2004). Modern Web search engines are designed to meet the needs of all users, regardless of their specific requirements. The retrieval of information for each user based on their preferences is referred to as personalization of Web search. The authors presented a novel approach to determining user profiles based on search histories. The user profiles are then used to improve the performance of Web search retrieval. A user profile and a common profile are created using the user's search history and a category hierarchy. The set of profiles is unified in order to map a user query into a group of categories that correspond to the user's search purpose and provide a context for deciphering the words in the user's query. Web searches are performed based on the user's query as well as the associations of the categories (Rose & Levinson, 2004). A fusion algorithm, as well as several profile learning and category mapping algorithms, are presented and reviewed. The strategy to personalizing Web search is quite effective, according to the results of the experiments. User profile results and tailored online search results were compared by J. Lai et al (Lai & Soh, 2005). On the internet, there is a vast amount of information. When a user searches for anything, it sometimes returns the same results for different types of queries. As a result, it is difficult for users to obtain meaningful and conclusive answers because it does not take into account user preferences or interests. Users' stated query search and (Lai & Soh, 2005) surfing actions are evaluated based on the searching query entered, the clicking rate of each link in the query result, and the time spent on the specific site. The solution is to develop a user searching profile as well as a method for developing document profiles. The evaluation concludes by demonstrating how to use this model to combine document and user searching profiles in order to provide users with relevant customized search results. According to Kraft et al., (Kraft et al., 2005) the context indicates any additional information linked with the question in the search box in its general mode, and they also describe alternative approaches to execute contextual search instead of modelling user profiles (Dourish, 2004). Search engines can employ context information to custom-tailor search results if it is provided by every user in any pattern, whether implicitly or explicitly, manually or automatically. A tailored search is the name given to the procedure. Personalized online search in this form could be client or server-based (T. T. S. Nguyen et al., 2013)

Flexible online search based on user profile was proposed by Sugiyama et al. (Rubens et al., 2015). The key benefit of this technique was that a user profile could be created without any effort or input from the user. The fundamental issue with the prior strategy is that it requires constant user communication. This strategy was successful in resolving the issue. When a user enters a search query to a search engine via a web browser, the search engine responds with search results that match the query. The user may choose a web page based on the search results in an attempt to meet their information needs. In addition, the user can access new web pages by clicking on the hyperlinks on the web pages they've already seen and browsing. The suggested system keeps track of a user's surfing history and automatically updates their profile anytime their browser page changes. The search results adapt based on the user's profile the next time they submit a query. Susmitha et al. developed an interface based solely on keywords for precise domain selection (Xu & Li, 2014). As a result, data is fragmented into distinct parameters that are only relevant to a specific domain. Keywords submitted by the user are also linked to a specific website, allowing the user to search for specific information. Some researchers concentrated on query grouping, which allows the search engine to comprehend the user's session (Mohamed & Hassan, 2008). When a query group is evaluated, a search engine can quickly determine the context of queries and clicks within that query group. A query group is a collection of inquiries submitted by the same user and tied to a common informational need. Query groups are dynamically updated when the user enters new queries, and new groups may be created over time. It looked at long-term search history, which is made up of past inquiries and can be used to improve retrieval performance. It is also demonstrated that such information can be useful in coordinating user search histories into query groups. Matthijs and Radlinski et al. use Firefox to collect web usage data such as the URL of the page, the date and time of the page session, the duration of the page visit, and the length of the source HTML (Matthijs & Radlinski, 2011). Peng et al. created a user profile by compiling search results that users had utilised with the help of the Google register. A tree is maintained in this architecture, and subjects are linked in the tree. The tree directory manages each topic that is searched by the user and kept in a tree structure. Link The number of visitors is kept track of, and it reflects the level of user interest. Christian Wagner et al. provided a general web log search result for re-ranking procedure that may be utilized to re-order search results utilizing the personalized ranking principle(Du & Wagner, 2006). The user's search history log or simply the modelling of user search attitude and interests can be used to study, learn, and create such criteria, which can then be implemented (Shafiq et al., 2015).

2.2.3 State of the art in personalized web page ranking

Because of the digital era, information retrieval has gotten a lot of interest in the research community. In the actual world, consumers are unaware of the exact keyword they will use to retrieve information. As a result, they are getting both relevant and irrelevant results. If a user does not know the exact keyword, they may see irrelevant results. The search engines of today are more powerful. To provide the best results to their users, they investigate the semantic relationships between words and use a variety of glossaries. Regardless of the fact that there is a chasm between man and machine. Human analysis and comprehension differ from computer analysis and comprehension in the sense that they are not the same. The machine should analyze and comprehend the users' information needs before providing the best service possible. The convergence of personalization, knowledge-based mining, and semantic web, according to this study, is transforming the old web scenario into web 3.0 (Rudman & Bruwer, 2016). As seen in Table 1, the majority of the authors prefer ontologies for customization (Sieg et al., 2007c, 2007b, 2007a),. In the subject of online usage mining, researchers are attempting to make machines think and analyze like humans using ontologies. Concepts are crucial in the construction of ontologies since they explain the contents of online publications explicitly. Exact concepts are used to improve the accuracy of the information retrieval process.

Based on our findings, we can conclude that using NLP to analyse the entire document enables us to personalize the website and extract the most relevant themes. When we analyse full documents offline and generate domain knowledge ontologies with extracted concepts, the response time of an Information Retrieval system is unaffected. By combining personalization with this method, we can provide the user with the desired and effective outcome. The most important aspect of information retrieval is providing the user with pertinent and necessary information. To do so, the machine must comprehend the following: what the user truly means, where it occurs, and how it occurs. Natural Language Processing techniques and ontologies are extremely useful in completing the task at hand (Chowdhury, 2003; Kao & Poteet, 2007). These are the conclusions drawn from a review of twenty-five research studies. Depending on the findings, we believe that adding information about a user's usage history can help provide an effective ranking of web pages based on the user's preferences. Machines should recognise what web documents and pages deal with and what the users are asking in order to provide a better personalised result to the user. The machine should be able to comprehend these two facts. For this, machines must think, understand, and make decisions in the same way that humans do. Ontologies and natural language processing techniques can help achieve this (Zaihrayeu et al., 2007).

In addition to these public relations strategies, we conducted a thorough comparison of the most recent page ranking methodologies that have been deployed in recent years from a variety of sources (2013 to 2019). We considered the following table-3 as a final apprehension of our study, which focuses on the strengths, limitations, and methodologies employed in each paper. Some of the strategies work well in certain situations, while others fall short. But, in the end, each of them has its own set of merits and characteristics.

Table 2.3 Various techniques for web user personalization

S.No	Approach used	Goal	Author(s)
1	Multi-variant k-means methods	Personalized URL Recommendation	Bamshad Mobasher

2	C/NC, TF, TF-IDF and personalized B25 weighting	Personalized search results from search Engine	Nicolaas Matthijis
3	Conceptual Term Frequency	Document Clustering	Ourdia Bouidghaghen et.al
4	Graph based Ontological similarity Measure	Personaliz1ation for Mobile Users	D.Dhanalakshmi et.al
5	Ontology representation and RSVM	Personalization for Mobile users	Christo foros Panayiotou et.al
6	XML Schema	Personalization for Mobile users	Kenneth Wai-Ting Leung and DikLun Lee
7	Natural Language Processing, Verb argument structure, Conceptual term frequency	Document Clustering	Alessandro Micarelli et.al
8	Bipartite graph, Personalized Agglomerative Clustering	Concept based user profiles	Jie Yu and Fangfang Liu
9	Bayesian learning	Recommendation of next travel location	Yan-Ying Chen et.al
10	Association Rule Interactive post-Procesusing Schemas and sing Ontologies	Interesting Association Rules	Thi Thanh Sang Nguyen
11	Ontology, Personalized page view (PPV) graph	Personalization (Preferred information in the shortest path)	VeeramalaiSankaradass and Kannan Arputharaj
12	Fuzzy-Temporal Association Rule Mining	Dynamic Personalization	Yunbo Cao, Jun Xu et.al

13	Bayesian learning and expectation-maximization (EM) techniques	Extracting Information from unseen websites	Shady Shehata, FakhriKarray
14	frequent patterns	Personalized search results from search Engine	Xiao-Bing Xue and Zhi-Hua Zhou
15	tfidf+ distributional features	Document Clustering	Claudia Marinica and FabriceGuillet
16	tree templates and schema	Extracting data from web pages	S.Sendhilkumar and T. V. Geetha
17	ontology-based, multi-facet (OMF) profile, RSVM	Personalized search results from search Engine	Tak-Lam Wong and Wai Lam
18	Ontology, semantic mining	Knowledge based information	Mohammed Kayed and Chia-Hui Chang
19	Ontology	Recommendation of web page, Personalization	Konstantin Todorov
20	Normalization	Web log Analysis	M. Jordan Raddick, Ani R. Thakar et.al
21	VSM, LDA model, Gibbs Sampling, BP-Growth Algorithm ,Maximum Entropy and Limited-Memory BFGS	classification	Hengshu Zhu, Enhong Chen et.al
22	Genetic Algorithm	Prioritizing Web Links Based on Web Usage and Content Data	K. Chaudhary and S. Gupta

23	Sequential Pattern Mining and Attribute Based Collaborative Filtering	Personalized Recommendation of Learning Material	M Salehi, IN Kamalabadi and MBG Ghoushchi
24	collaborative filtering (CF), sequential pattern mining (SPM)	Recommend learning items in users' learning processes.	W Chen, Z Niu, X Zhao and Y Li

Table 2.4 Comparative view of different Page ranking approaches used in current state of art

Year	Author	Approach	Pros	Cons
2013	Derhami V	Rank of the pages has been decided by Simple Collaborative filtering	Similarity of users preferences are the primary consideration to quantify ranks of web pages.	Improper web ranking under this scheme in spite of having been emphatically worried about the web query.
2014	Roobam and Vallimayli	CF is utilized over memory uses Improvement to interpret page ranking	CF based outcome is utilized while preprocessing on site pages to accomplish reasonable page rank for	New website pages go positioned hopelessly under this plan Despite the fact that they are profoundly worried about the web inquiry.

Year	Author	Approach	Method	Limitation
			the pertinent query.	
2015	Kaviarasan et al	Collaborative filtering approach has been applied utilizing K-Mean Clustering to settle on positioning of pages.	Recommendation strategies to improve page rank in setting to web search query.	While assigning the page rank, it has been demonstrated insufficient while managing new website pages for a same query
2015	Moreno et al.	Collaborative filtering is utilized in arrangement and affiliation rules for concluding the page rank.	Hybrid Recommendation system and Ontology approach is used decide on page ranks w.r.t. user's query	Does not yield promising outcomes on shifted and complex inquiry by various clients with new queries.
2015	Bairagade et al.	Web Crawler approach is referenced for improvising page rank.	Documents are preprocessed while crawling in web.	Unable to improve page ranking modules.
2016	Sharma and Lodhi	ML (Machine Learning) and DT (Decision Tree) approaches are used to rank the pages.	User's Logs are referenced Traditional machine Learning method used for page ranking	Fall short off on other Applicable machine learning techniques

| 2017 | Aqlan et al. | Artificial neural Network with regression technique used for page ranking. | Advanced AI methods used for improving page ranking algorithms. | Does Not utilized any other traditional AI techniques in page ranking that has positive impact. |

The above table summarized view of different page ranking algorithm approaches by addressing advantages and disadvantages. The strengths, shortcomings, and approaches employed in each paper are depicted in Table 2.4. Some of the strategies work well in certain situations, while others fall short. UIS outperforms all other algorithms and yields promising results in tailored web search. As a result, Page Rank has been determined from the desired network profile based on user interest scores. Without the user's input, user preferences and selections are categorized and tracked. At last, search results are shown to users on the matching results that are mapped.

2.3 Conclusion

The above algorithms are effective at retrieving web pages from search engines. The link analysis techniques are based on the document's link structure. The retrieval performance of a page with many links and references can be improved. Personalized web search is included in the integrated ranking strategy. The material and the connection are both combined in an integrated method to improve retrieval efficiency. Page segmentation techniques are used to divide a page into blocks, and by doing so, retrieval performance in the web environment can be enhanced. Each algorithm has its own set of advantages and disadvantages. We can use the above-mentioned algorithms to meet the needs of a search engine. It aids in the enhancement of Google's current page rank algorithm, and these web page ranking methods might be utilized by a variety of different search engines to increase the retrieval efficiency of online sites based on the user's query.

Data mining is a term used to describe strategies for extracting a little bit of usable data from a huge amount of data (H. Li et al., 2017). Traditional yet two most popular data mining approaches, first association rule mining and another classical rule mining, have been combined to improve efficiency. Associative classification is the name of the new method (López-Sánchez et al., 2019). Classification rule mining is a technique for identifying a limited collection of rules in a database that can be utilized to create an accurate classifier. Association rule mining identifies all rules in a database that meet certain minimal support and confidence requirements. The discovery objective for association rule mining is not predetermined, whereas there is only one predetermined target for classification rule mining.

If the two mining processes can be combined in any way, the user will benefit from significant cost savings and ease. Here, the integration is accomplished by the use of on a subset of association rules whose right-hand side is limited to the categorization class attribute, the above mentioned combination is accomplished by working on a subset of association rules formally known as class association rules (CARs) (Wenmin Li et al., 2001; L. T. T. Nguyen et al., 2013). Traditional classification algorithms offer higher accuracy but slower speeds than the new combined approach associative classification. Associative categorization is done in a variety of ways (Zhu et al., 2016). The goal of this research is to compare all of the major associative categorization techniques. Although a prior study of this type was completed (Fernández-Navarro et al., 2016), numerous new work has been done and published in this sector since then. As a result of this research, a greater grasp of the current status of associative categorization approaches will be gained. The following is a quick overview of associative classification.

There aren't many associations in a transactional database used for association rule mining. While categorization data typically has a large number of relationships. To avoid combinatorial explosion, an adaptation of the existing association rule mining algorithm to mine only the CARs is required. A variation of the current existing association rule mining algorithm to mine mainly the CARs is required (Wenmin Li et al., 2001). This variation involves discretizing persistent qualities in view of a picked class point in the classification. The primary problems of the current frameworks are tackled as beneath.

1. Understandability problem: The rules created by standard order frameworks are commonly hard to comprehend. Also, numerous understandable rules are left unseen.

2. Interesting rule problem: In request to get a little arrangement of rules of the current existing classification frameworks brings about many interesting and helpful rules not being found.

3. Memory Problem: All conventional arrangement frameworks require stacking the entire dataset into main memory. In any event, the database can remain under the circle rather than the main memory in this manner.

3.1 Associative Classification

Associative Classification (AC) is a typical classification learning strategy in data mining that builds categorization models using association rule discovery approaches and classification (Abdelhamid & Thabtah, 2014). AC is a special case of the association rule in which the target attribute is taken into account on the right-hand side of the rule (Ventura & Luna, 2018). For example, in a rule like: C must be the target attribute, the input, the training data set D includes a number of separate attributes A, A2..., An, and C is the target attribute, the training data set D has a number of unique attributes A, A2..., An, and C is the target attribute (class). Nominal attributes (those with a limited range of possible values) and continuous attributes (those with an infinite range of possible values) are both feasible (real or integer). To convert continuous attributes to categorical attributes, they should be discretized using a discretization algorithm. The minimum support (Min Supp) and minimum confidence (Min Conf) levels are the most critical in associative categorization (Min Conf). Minimum support is calculated by dividing the size of the training data set by the frequency of the attribute value and its associated class. Minimum confidence represents the frequency of the attribute value and its corresponding class in the training data set as a percentage of the frequency of that attribute value in that training data set. The frequent ruleitem is an attribute value with an associated class that passes Min Supp, frequent 1- ruleitem is a single-attribute frequent ruleitem, frequent 2- ruleitem is a two-attribute frequent ruleitem, and so on. In general, there are three phases to an AC algorithm. AC looks for hidden correlations between attribute values and class attribute values in the training data set in the first phase. Once all of the frequently used ruleitems have been identified, "Class Association Rules" (CARs) are generated in a "if-then" structure. The ranking and trimming operations begin in the second phase. At this point, CARs are rated according to a set of metrics, such as confidence and support values, to ensure that rules with high confidence are prioritized for inclusion in the classifier (Al-Hawari et al., 2020; Pejman, 2012). However, because the number of rules generated is in the hundreds, and many of them are redundant and do not discriminate across classes, rule pruning is required to remove the contradictory and redundant rules from the entire collection of CARs. The set of CARs that represents the final classifier model is the outcome of the second step. Finally, the classification model is used to forecast class values on previously unknown data (test data).

3.2 Associative Classification Process

CBA (Classification Based on Associations) is a convergence analysis-based ordered rule method (X. Lu et al., 2007). It is divided into two sections. CBA-RG is a rule generator for finding association rules based on the Apriori method (Al-Maolegi & Arkok, 2014). A classifier builder, CBA-CB, produces classifiers from the rules generated by the CBA-RG in the second half. CBA generates all candidate rules, which are association rules with specific support and confidence levels. Then it chooses a tiny subset of the rules to create a classifier. The best rule is used for classification when predicting the class label of the example with the highest level of confidence. The data is scanned numerous times in the CBA-RG method (Gambhir & Gondaliya, 2012). All of the frequently used rule items are generated in these many passes. It counts the support in the first pass and evaluates if it is frequent or not. The seed set of rules developed and found to be frequent in the previous pass is used in each future iteration. It uses this data to build candidate rules, which are new potentially frequent rules. During the pass, the actual support for these candidate rules is computed. It determines which of the candidate rule items are genuinely frequent and can yield CARs at the conclusion of the pass. The CBA-CB method was utilized to create a CAR-based classifier (Y. J. Wang et al., 2008, 2007). To create the best classifier, all of the available subsets of the training data are evaluated, and the subset with the proper rule sequence and the fewest errors is chosen. The following are the approach's limitations:

• It generates a large number of mined rules, resulting in computational cost.

The classification is based on a single, high-confidence rule that may be skewed. CMAR is a non-profit organization dedicated to (Classification based on Multiple Association Rules) Because the classification is based on a single high-confidence rule, the associative classification suffers from a large number of mining rules, which can lead to biased classification or overfitting. CMAR (Classification based on Multiple Association Rules) is a suggested associative classification approach in which classification is accomplished based on a weighted analysis employing multiple strong association rules (Zaki et al., 2020). A weighted X2 analysis with numerous strong association criteria is used to classify the data. CBA has various flaws as well, as shown below.

• First, determining the most effective rule for classifying a new case is difficult.

• Second, a large number of rules is frequently generated from a training data set.

Instead, then relying on a single rule for categorization, a set of rules is used to decide the class label. A new approach called weighted X2 is being developed to avoid prejudice. It derives a decent measure of how strong the rule is under both conditional support and class distribution. CMAR uses a unique data structure known as the CR-tree to store and retrieve a large number of classification rules in a compact and efficient way, which improves both accuracy and efficiency. CMAR accelerates the mining of a complete set of rules by employing a variant of the recently published FP-growth algorithm, which is significantly quicker than Apriori-like methods.

The CMAR process is divided into two stages: rule generation and classification. CMAR helps to generate a comprehensive rule sets in the form R: P -> C, where P- pattern in the available and used training data set & C- Class label such that sup (R) and conf (R) pass the appropriate support and confidence levels. Additionally, CMAR trimsfew rules and able to only classifies a subset of high-quality rules. In the subsequent second step, CMAR further extracts a subset of rules that match the object and analyses this subset of rules to anticipate the item's class label. It is classed if all of the rules produce the same class designation (Wenmin Li et al., 2001).

3.3 Association-Rule Mining Algorithm

The Association rules quality is tried to be discovered throughout the rule discovery process and also determines the accuracy of associative classification. Numerous association rule mining techniques are available to mine-up frequent data sets in a database transaction. Apriori, frequent pattern (FP) growth, Equivalence Class Transformation (Eclat), Dynamic Itemset Counting (DIC), Partition, and others are some of the most prominent association rule mining techniques. We used the Apriori (Yuan, 2017) method to classify and construct the rules in our research.

3.3.1 Apriori algorithm

The recognizable proof of incessant itemsets is directed in various stages in the Apriori algorithm of association rule mining (Agrawal et al., 1993), with each progression utilizing itemsets distinguished as regular in the first means to produce a bunch of new competitor itemsets. The 'downward-closure' part of the algorithm is utilized to accelerate the hunt interaction by decreasing the number of up-and-comer itemsets at each progression. The 'downward-closure' characteristic guarantees that every subset containing an oftentimes happening itemset is likewise regularly happening. If an itemset is infrequent at any point during the process, it will be ignored and deleted from the list of frequently occurring itemsets. This feature is used by the Apriori algorithm to discover and eliminate candidate itemsets with infrequent subsets. Prior to counting the help worth of itemsets at any stage, this pruning is finished. The time it takes to create itemsets and work out the help an incentive for all mixes of things in the conditional database is reduced as a result of this managing strategy (F. Thabtah, 2007; F. A. Thabtah & Cowling, 2007).

3.3.2 Frequent Pattern growth algorithm

CMAR, proposed by W. Li (Wenmin Li et al., 2001) uses methodologies based on the frequent pattern (FP)-growth method explained by J Han et al. to improve the efficiency of the Apriori candidate generation stage (Wenmin Li et al., 2001). The FP-tree is created using the FP-growth method. The training data set was used to create this dense tree. This tree is implicit in such a way that each training element compares to the unique tree's paths. Therefore, the length of every path is addressed by the all-outnumber of continuous objects relating to it in the tree. For the accompanying reasons, this kind of portrayal is very significant.

1. The FP-tree reflects all of the frequent itemsets from the transactional database, which decreases storage requirements because the FP-tree is smaller than the original transactional database because frequent items share a lot of information.

2. The FP-tree can be inherent just two stages, with the initial step creating successive itemsets and their backing esteem in every exchange. The FP-tree is inherent the subsequent stage.

After the FP-tree has been fabricated, the rules are found utilizing an example development approach that utilizations patterns of unit length in the FP-tree. All extra likely successive patterns existing with it in the FP-tree are perceived and saved in a contingent FP-tree for each continuous example recognized. Connecting the patterns produced by the 50 contingent FP-tree is utilized to play out the mining. The FP-development strategy utilizes an alternate mining technique than the Apriori algorithm; there is no competitor rule creation in the FP-development strategy. One of the huge downsides of the FP-development procedure is that there is no assurance that the FP-tree will forever fit in main memory, particularly when the objective database is immense.

3.3.3 Greedy Method

The FOIL (First Order Inductive Learner) algorithm was developed by J R Quinlan and R Cameron-Jones (Quinlan & Cameron-Jones, 1993). The FOIL algorithm uses the FOIL-gain approach to heuristically create rules from training literals, also known as items, for each class in the training data set. The FOIL-gain approach assesses the data acquired by adding a condition to the present rule. The FOIL algorithm looks for the literal in the training data set that yields the largest FOIL-gain for a specific class. All training objects associated with that literal are eliminated once it is detected, and the operation is repeated until all positive data objects for the current class are covered. This procedure is carried out for each of the classes.

3.3.4 Confidence Rules

The association rule discovery mechanism and the 'Association Classification' Techniques of data mining are based on the support threshold.' Rules that have confidence value in highly number being frequently ignored due to insufficient support values. A support threshold value is typically used to limit the amount of rules generated. Because the support value is less than the threshold, this technique is sometimes unable to catch rules with high confidence values. To conquer this constraint and search an enormous pursuit space to catch whatever a number of high-confidence rules could be allowed, the overall methodology is to decrease the worth of the help limit. Nonetheless, this can now and then bring about issues, for example, over-fitting, the development of rules with measurably low help esteems, and countless probable competitor rules requiring a ton of CPU time and storage. To address this problem, K Wang et al. (K. Wang et al., 2002) suggested a method for generating association rules that just employs the confidence threshold value and defers the support threshold (K. Wang et al., 2007, 2001). As per Wang's approach, the minimum confidence thresholds value is used to find the rules of data collected. The support threshold is not mandatory now in the candidate generation phase, according to R. Agrawal et al. (Agrawal et al., 1993). The support-based approaches use 'downward-closure' property is now not so worthy. Due to the reason that the downward-closure attribute relies on the support threshold to eliminate infrequent candidate itemsets and minimize needless support computation, it can't be used because the support threshold is suspended (F. Thabtah, 2007).

3.4 Problems with Associative Classification

The extensive search in a very wide search space of viable rules is one of the major drawbacks of employing association rule mining in Association Classification techniques. As a result, discovering association rules is computationally expensive, especially when using tiny support thresholds, which are required for training efficient associative classifiers from big datasets. The second difficulty is that traditional Association Classification approaches do not properly combine the rule discovery and classification processes. Traditionally, these processes have been carried out individually, which may have an impact on the classification process's predictive effectiveness (T D Do, 2009).

3.5 Associative Classification Schemes

Associative classification (AC) is an associated filed of data mining and widely utilized in research. In the rule discovery process, association rule mining is utilized by associative classification uses extract efficient rules that can precisely generalize the training data set. Association classification systems have been proved as highly accurate when compared to other classification approaches (T D Do, 2009).

The classifier is built using association rules that are identified and assessed in associative classification. The idea is that by looking at these association rules, we may see if there are any existence of strong links between class labels & common patterns (Attribute conjunctions value pairs). Due to availability of highly confident correlations across several characteristics in association rules, they can overcome the restrictions of decision-tree induction, which only employs one characteristic at a time. In research, associative classification has been shown to be more precise than other traditional classification methods. In this report, the following methods will be discussed: CBA, CMAR, and CPAR (Wenmin Li et al., 2001; B. Liu et al., 1998; Yin & Han, 2003).

3.5.1 Classification Based on Association (CBA)

The CBA is made up of two parts. The first half is a rule generator (named CBA-RG) that finds association rules from the training data set using the Apriori technique, and the second half is a classifier builder (called CBA-CB).

- CBA-main RG's goal is to locate all rule-items having a support level greater than the support threshold. Ruleitems that reach the support criterion are called frequent ruleitems, whereas those that do not are called rare ruleitems. As the promising rule to represent this set of rules, the rule with the highest confidence among all the rules with the same set of 53 components is chosen. We choose one rule at random when there are numerous rules with the same greatest confidence. We assert that the rule is true if the confidence value exceeds the confidence threshold. As a consequence, any promising rules that are frequent and have a confidence value larger than the confidence threshold are included in the list of class association rules.

- By completing several runs over the training data, the CBA-RG algorithm produces all of the frequent rules. To begin, it assesses the support value of each particular rule to determine whether or not the rule is frequent. In subsequent passes, it starts with the original set of frequent rules found in the previous pass. It generates new frequent rules from this initial set of rules, which are known as candidate rules. The actual support values for these candidate rules are calculated over the training data. At the end of each pass, the Class Association Rules are determined by determining the most frequent rules among the candidate rules (CARs) (L. T. T. Nguyen et al., 2013).
- The core principle of the CBA classifier building technique is to select a set of high precedence rules from all possible rules to cover the training data.

3.5.2 Classification Based on Multiple Association Rules (CMAR)

This algorithm has the following characteristics:

CMAR employs a group of rules for categorization rather than a single rule with the highest level of confidence. In CMAR, we select a small set of very precise (high confidence value) rules that are related to one another. The connection between these rules is being investigated. In general, CMAR outperforms CBA in terms of prediction accuracy.

CMAR makes use of CRtree (Wenmin Li et al., 2001) to improve accuracy and efficiency by storing a large number of rule-items compactly and allowing for efficient retrieval of these rules for classification.

CMAR employs a variant of the FP-growth method to accelerate the mining of the entire set of created item-rules. This method is significantly faster than Apriori or other traditional methods (W Li et al., 2001).

3.5.3 Classification Based on Predictive Association Rules (CPAR)

CPAR makes use of the following features to improve its accuracy and efficiency: CPAR uses dynamic programming to prevent having to repeat calculations for rule generation. Instead of selecting simply the greatest literal, all literals that are near to the best are chosen for rule creation. As a result, important rules will not be overlooked.

In comparison to classical association classification, CPAR is more efficient since it derives a smaller set of rules with higher accuracy and less redundancy.

3.6 Steps in Associative Classification

The development of a classifier employing Associative Classification can be broken down into four stages.

Phase 1: All frequent rule items are derived based on the support threshold in this phase.

Phase 2: All of the exact and effective association rules are generated in this phase. This is accomplished by picking from the list of frequent rules generated in step 1 those rules with a confidence value greater than the confidence threshold.

Phase 3: To construct the classifier, a subset of the association rules derived in phase 2 is chosen.

Phase 4: The performance of the constructed classifier is evaluated in this phase by running it on Test data items.

3.7 Evaluation Techniques

The test data set is used to evaluate the constructed classifier's performance. Performance evaluation is a crucial duty because it determines how effective the classification system is. The system is deemed to function well and be accepted if it delivers accurate classification of the training data set in the majority of situations. However, if the system provides numerous results in which the test data object is incorrectly categorized, we reject it. Many assessment methods have been proposed to evaluate the performance of the classifier, including error-rate (Witten & Frank, 2016), recall-precision (Eibe et al., 2016), and recall-precision (Van Rijsbergen, 1979).

1. To evaluate the efficacy of their classifiers, associative classification algorithms use the error-rate method (Witten & Frank, 2016). The error rate of a classifier is a measure of its predicted accuracy. The classification system is run on the test data in this way, and the classifier simply calculates the test data object classifications. It will be considered a success if the system correctly predicts the class. If the classifier incorrectly classifies a test object, it is considered an error. The overall error rate of a classifier is calculated by dividing the total number of error cases by the total number of cases in a test data set.

Another evaluation method utilized in classification applications such as Information Retrieval Systems is Precision and Recall (Van Rijsbergen, 1979). Work on precision and recall in the following manner. The IR system retrieves a document to satisfy the 56-query given a query. Some of the documents returned are relevant to the query, while others are not. Precision refers to the percentage of documents/answers that were successfully obtained by the system out of all those that were retrieved. The proportion of correctly recovered documents/answers by the system out of all right documents/answers is measured by recall. 3. To quantify the performance of all classes in multi-class and multi-label issues, precision and recall approaches must be coupled. As a result, in IR and text classification, a hybrid method dubbed F1 (Abdelhamid & Thabtah, 2014) has been utilized, which assesses the average effect of both precision and recall together. 4. For binary classification with two classes in the training data set, Provost et al. introduced a standard method termed a confusion matrix, which takes into consideration the cost of incorrect prediction (Provost & Kohavi, 1998). A confusion matrix, like precision and recall techniques, contains information about the classifier's actual and anticipated classifications. The data in the matrix is typically used to evaluate the performance of the generated classifier (Gu et al., 2009).

3.8 Conclusion

We covered the basics of association classification and association rule mining techniques in this chapter. These methods are extremely useful for classifying an entity based on its relationships with other entities in the context. Some academics employ the notion of association rule mining to optimize and refine the created rules. In Chapter 5, we'll look at how these rule sets are optimized using the BAT optimization process, which was inspired by nature.

4.1 Nature Inspired Optimization Techniques

Due to the fast speed of industrialization, engineering problem becomes more complex and difficult to optimize. These complex problems involve a large number of dimensions, variables, time, and space complexities. To tackle such a situation, nature-inspired algorithms are used to find the optimized solution to such problems. Nature Inspired computing techniques mimics the processes that exist in nature. These computing techniques are represented as an algorithm in the literature, and the collection of this algorithm is called nature-inspired algorithms. These algorithms use randomization bases approach, which permits them to find the solution after using construction steps in an iterative manner. These algorithms are user friendly because updating objective function as well as the

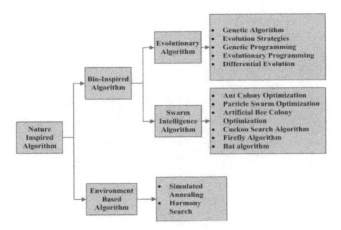

Figure 4.1 Classification of Nature inspired Optimization Techniques

implementation of the algorithm is easy. This feature of nature-inspired algorithm enables them as a good candidate for finding the solution to diverse types of problems prevailing in the research and application. Nature-inspired algorithms are general purpose algorithms that can be used to find the solution of different kind of problems. To achieve this goal, the primary requirement is to find appropriate tuning of the parameter to map the problem in hand.

4.1.1 Categorization of Nature-Inspired Algorithms

The nature-inspired algorithm can be categorized into two categories, bio-inspired algorithm and environment based (physics/chemistry) algorithms. Binitha and S. S. Sathya. (2012). Bio-inspired algorithms are inspired by the biological process that prevailed in the literature, e.g., the behavior of animals and plants. Bioinspired algorithms can also be divided into two types of algorithms based on evolution and swarm intelligence. A broad classification of nature-inspired algorithms is shown in the Figure 4.1. Evolutionary algorithms are inspired by the principle of survival of the fittest given by Charles Darwin and based on nature's evolution process. These algorithms use the concept of recombination and mutation operators for the optimization of complex engineering problems. The Genetic Algorithm (Holland, 1992) and Differential Evolution algorithm (Dorigo et al., 2006; Qin et al., 2008) are examples of such algorithms. Swarm intelligence-based algorithm mimics the collective behavior of the swarm presents in nature and finds the optimal solution of the complex engineering problems. Ant Colony Optimization algorithm (Karaboga & Basturk, 2007), Particle Swarm Optimization algorithm (Shi & Eberhart, 1999), Artificial Bee Colony Optimization algorithm (Heraguemi et al., 2014) are some examples of the algorithm based on swarm intelligence.

4.1.2 Particle Swarm Optimization Algorithm

Particle Swarm Optimization (PSO) algorithm is a rather effective algorithm based on swarm intelligence optimization. and has been used for finding the optimal solution for a wide range of application areas. This algorithm was developed by J. Kennedy (Kennedy & Eberhart, 1995). This algorithm simulates the swarm's foraging behavior of bird folks and schooling of fishes. It is a stochastic population-based, easy to implement, and effective optimization technique. In this approach, each particle (bird) has two things position and velocity. The position of each particle represents a solution to the problem in hand. This algorithm also maintains the five parameters particle's velocity, particle's position, a current globally best position achieved by the particles, individual's particle's best position so far, and best position by the neighbor particle. In each iteration, particles update their position as well as its velocity until all particles converge on some point or termination condition is reached. The algorithm begins with the initial random population. This population is referred to as swarm, and the swarm scans the problem's domain and seeks the best answer according to the algorithm implementation criteria. The following three elements are used to move the particles in the search space. First is the current velocity of the particle. Second, the particle's distance from its best location so far, and third, the particle's distance from the best position so far. All particles of the swarm share their findings among each other by communicating its position to other particles. There are two components in the trajectory of the particle. One component is deterministic, and the other is stochastic. For a d dimensional search space, the particle's position is denoted by Xi, and velocity is denoted by Vi. Each particle in a d-dimensional space is represented by a d-dimensional positional vector $Xi = [Xi1, Xi2,...,Xid]$, and all particles are referred to as the population. P_{best} is the particle's previous best value, and it is defined as Pbesti = [Pbesti1, Pbesti2,...,Pbestid]. The best value of each particle is referred to as the global best (Pgbest) and is denoted by Pgbesti = [Pgbesti1, Pgbesti2,..., Pgbesti1d]. The particle's velocity is defined as $Vi = [Vi1, Vi2,..., Vid]$.

Based on the two equations above, the population of particles converges on a global best solution while each particle moves at random. PSO Algorithm is more efficient than evolutionary algorithms like GA. This is because PSO is far more versatile than GA in search space exploration.

In the literature, approximately 30 different versions are present. All these versions are built to remove some weaknesses in the algorithm and as per the requirement of the problem to be solved. Among these versions of the PSO, the classic PSO algorithm is simple to apply and uses less parameters. Figure 4.2 shows the flowchart of the PSO.

4.1.3 Ant Colony Optimization Algorithm

Ant Colony Optimization algorithm (ACO) is also among the most prominently used population and meta heuristic-based nature-inspired algorithms. This algorithm is developed by Marco Dorigo in 1999. This algorithm simulates the foraging process of ants. Ant seeks the shortest path from food source to nest. Initially, ants move in random directions, and once ants find the food source, it brings that food to their nest by following the shortest route. This shortest route is established by the ants themselves by using a special chemical substance called pheromone (Dorigo & Stützle, 2019). When ant returns to the nest after collecting food, it segregates pheromone on the path followed by it. This pheromone attracts other ants to follow that path. Other ants also segregate some pheromone when they travel that path. Such action raises pheromone concentration on the shortest route, encouraging more ants to pursue such direction. This cycle continues until all ants of the same nest follow that shortest route. When the food source is exhausted, ant's movement on that path reduces, which leads to the low concentration of the pheromone because it evaporates over time. Low concentration of the pheromone discourages other ants to follow that path. In this situation, ants explore some other area for the collection of the food. The algorithm based on the above-mentioned approach uses three functions, construct Ant Solution, pheromone Update, and demon Action.

Construct Ant Solution: This function constructs the solution by simulating the movement of ants and build the solution in an iterative manner.

Pheromone Update: This function is used to increase the concentration of the pheromone by deposit more pheromone as well as decrease the concentration of the pheromone by evaporating it.

Demon Action: This function is optional and depends on the problem that has to be solved. It is used to deposit the pheromone in a biased manner.

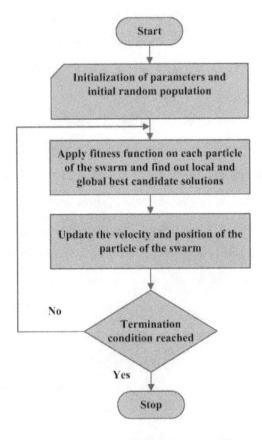

Figure 4.2 Flow diagram of PSO Algorithm

Optimal route-finding in the computer network, wireless sensor network, traveling salesman problem, vehicular routing, and automatic voltage regulation are some examples of the areas in which ACO has been used effectively.

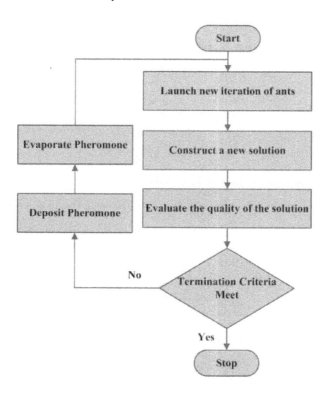

Figure 4.3 Flow chart of ACO algorithm

Although there is a problem of premature convergence in the ACO algorithm because pheromone concentration changes with time and there are some parameters, e.g., pheromone quantity, pheromone updating rule, and rate of the evaporation, which requires proper tuning as per the requirement of the problem. Flowchart of the ACO algorithm is shown in the Figure 4.3.

4.1.4 Cuckoo Search Algorithm

Cuckoo Search Algorithm (CSA) is based on the brood parasitic nature of some cuckoo species. This algorithm mimics the breeding procedure of these cuckoos. The cuckoo lays its egg in the nest of some other bird by choosing the nest in a very clever way. It selects only those nests in which the host bird laid her eggs recently, and the color or texture of these eggs resembles with the cuckoo egg. If the host bird detects the cuckoo's eggs, it either moves cuckoo's eggs outside the nest or either leaves its own nest and builds a new one somewhere else. If the host bird does not recognize the cuckoo eggs, in this case, the cuckoo egg hatches faster than the host bird's eggs. When cuckoo chicks come out from the egg, it propelled down the other eggs outside the nest by simply following its natural instinct. Some chicks of the cuckoo also mimic the voice of the host bird's chicks. These two behaviors of the cuckoo chicks guarantee that the cuckoo chicks get the most of the food supplied by the host bird. This cuckoo activity is stimulated by two researchers, (X.-S. Yang, 2010) and (Roy & Chaudhuri, 2013).

As per CSA, cuckoo chose a nest randomly from a fixed number of available eggs and lay a single egg in a nest. While cuckoo can lay more than one egg at a time in some updated versions of this algorithm. The egg laid by the cuckoo can be marked by the host bird at the probability P_a [0,1]. In this algorithm, the egg in the nest is a solution to the problem, and the egg that has just been placed is a fresh solution to the problem. If the new solution provided by the cuckoo is better than the available solutions, then the worst solution available in the nest is replaced by the new solution. CSA uses the following three rules for the solution of the optimization problem

a) The cuckoo lays a single egg at a time in a randomly selected nest.

b) The nest, which has a better quality of the egg is carried forward to the future generation of the solution.

c) The host bird is likely to recognize the cuckoo egg by probability p_a [0,1]. In this situation, the host bird can simply leave the nest or move the cuckoo egg out of the nest.

4.2 Virtual BAT Algorithm

Xin–She Yang (2010) developed the standard BAT algorithm based on the echolocation or bio sonar individuality of micro bats. There are over a thousand different types of bats. Their sizes can range from tiny bumble bee bats weighing 1.5 to 2 grammes to massive bats with a 2m wide span and weighing up to 1 kg. The majority of the bat's echolocation occurs to some extent. Micro bats, more than any other species, rely heavily on echolocation, whereas mega bats do not. Micro bats typically use echolocation, a type of sonar, to detect prey, avoid obstacles, and navigate in the dark (Ervural et al., 2017). They can fire an extremely loud sound pulse and then listen for the echo that rebounds back from adjacent objects. The properties of pulses differ depending on the species and can be linked to the species' hunting strategy. Most bats use short, frequency modulated signals to sweep through an octave, with each pulse lasting tens of thousands of seconds (up to 8 to 10 ms) in the frequency range of 25KHz to 150KHz.

When searching for prey, micro bats can emit 10 to 20 such sound bursts per second, and the rate of pulse emission can be increased to 200 pulses per second. Because the speed of sound in air is approximately v=340m/s, the wavelength of ultrasonic sound bursts with a constant frequency is given in the range of 2mm to 14mm for a typical frequency range of 25KHz to 150KHz. These wave lengths correspond to the sizes of their prey. The BAT algorithm is a new swarm intelligent optimization technique inspired by bat social behavior and the phenomenon of echolocation to sense distance. BATs are normally fascinating animals. They have a high level of echolocation ability.

4.2.1 Encoding and Fitness function

The rules discovered through Apriori algorithm have been refined using BAT algorithm, a nature inspired optimization technique.

Yang used three generalized rules to convert bat behavior to algorithm:

- All bats use echolocation to sense distance and, in some mysterious way, they can tell the difference between food and background barriers.
- Bats search for prey by flying randomly with velocity vi at position xi at a fixed frequency fmin, varying wavelength, and loudness A0.
- Although the loudness can vary in a variety of ways, we assume that it ranges from a positive large value A0 to a minimum constant value. $A min$

We treated each rule as a chromosome of k+1 length for implementation purposes, with the 0th position serving as the cut point separating the antecedent and consequent of the rule. Positions 1 to k are the index of the items, Let the rule $X \Longrightarrow Y$, $X = (A_1, A_2, \ldots, A_j)$ and $Y = (A_{j+1}, A_{j+2}, \ldots, A_k)$ is encoded as:

J	I_1	I_2	....	I_j	I_{j+1}	.....	I_n

Let the rule

$p3 \wedge p4 \wedge p2 \wedge p8 \Longrightarrow p5$, will be represented as:

5	0	3	1	2	6	0	0	4	0	0	0	0	0

$p1 \wedge p8 \wedge p11 \wedge p13 \wedge p7 \Longrightarrow P9$, will be represented as:

6	1	0	0	0	0	0	5	2	7	0	3	0	4	0

Fitness Function: We calculated the fitness of each rule based on the rules support and confidence value as proposed by (Heraguemi et al., 2015). (Here a & b are empirical parameters with a=1, b=1).

$$f(R) = \begin{cases} \frac{[a.conf(R)+b.supp(R)]}{a+b} & if\ rule\ accepted \\ -1 & otherwise \end{cases} \quad (4.1)$$

Based on the fitness value, the initial population (set of best rules is obtained from the rules generated through Apriori algorithm).

4.2.2 Frequency and Velocity

Frequency f_i: Frequency represents the number of items in a rule which can be changed. Hence the maximum frequency can be f_{max} can be the total number of items in the dataset whereas minimum frequency f_{min} can be 0.

The frequency is updated in iteration k by using the formula:

$$f_{new} = 1 + \mu \cdot f_{max} \quad (4.2)$$

Where μ is a random value from the set [0,1]

Velocity:

In our approach velocity represents the position where a change may occur. The velocity parameter is updated in iteration k using the following formula:

$$v_{new} = f_{max} - f_{new} - v_{old} \quad (4.3)$$

4-2.3 Finding Global Best

In our implementation, position are the rules. The position (rules) are updated in iteration k using the steps discussed in.

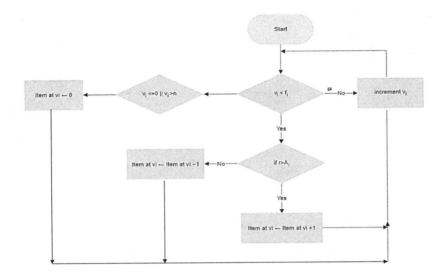

Figure 4.4 Flow chart of virtual BAT motion implementation

Steps for implementing BAT motion:

    while (v_i< Frequency f_i) do

    if ($r > A_i$) then   # r is random value and A is average loudness

    Item at v_i ←— Item at v_i+1   # item at position v_i + 1 position is shifted to position v_i

    else

    Item at v_i ←— Item at v_i−1   # item at position v_i - 1 position is shifted to position v_i

    end if

    if (Item at v_i is less or equal to 0 or greater than number of items) then

    Item at v_i ←— 0

    end if

    increment v_i

    end while

4.3 Conclusion

In this chapter we have discussed many nature inspired optimization techniques for finding best global solution. Every strategy has its pros and cons. In our research we have selected BAT algorithm for the optimization of rules got from Apriory algorithm. Selection of BAT algorithm is based on its simplicity of its implementation and flexibility. Beside above points we have summarized three attributes frequency tuning, automatic zooming and parameter control for selecting BAT algorithm for finding optimal solution.

The web page personalization based on web mining technique has two major phases, offline and online. The objective of the offline phase is to model user's navigation pattern using the history, web log data. This model is used to predict a user navigation pattern and give recommendations to them based on prediction.

We have collected implicit user information. Implicit data is the past user activity data which automatically stored in web server logs without their knowledge.

Web log file includes a variety of information depending on their nature and source; however, the most frequent log files contain the following:

- **IP address of user**: Unique IP address is assigned to each user.
- **Time stamp and Date**: Information regarding the date and time of user's request.
- **Request mode**: User's request like GET, POST and HEAD.
- **IP address of remote host**: This determines unique client on web.
- **Requested URL**: This determines the web pages requested by user.
- **States**: States codes like as 200, 404, and 203 are returned by the server to the client.
- **Bytes:** Content of information about transferred data.
- **Agent type**: User agent information.
- **Remote URL**: User's navigational behavior.
- **Page last visited:** The user's last page on the site before leaving.

5.1 Proposed system

In this research work, we have proposed a hybrid approach based on optimized association mining rule to get the ranking of webpages.

The concept of Association Rule Mining is used to get the association (most frequent occurring item set) between the webpages. Association rules generated reflects the possibilities that if a user access a certain set of webpages then he/she will also access a particular webpage. These rules are then optimized using BAT algorithm, a nature inspired approach(X.-S. Yang, 2010). The steps involved in the proposed system are represented in figure 5.1.

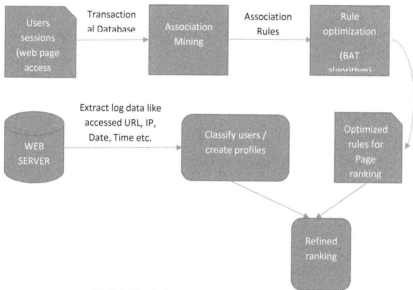

Fig 5.1. Block diagram of the proposed system

5.2 Data Set

In this work 2 different datasets were used. Initially a private dataset D1 was used for the training & testing of the system. For validation purpose a baseline dataset D2 was used our work.

5.2.1 Dataset D1

For the purpose of training and testing the system we have taken data from a webserver of a multinational organization in Gurugram. This is not a public dataset, but the organization agreed to share the web server log provided that we must agree and ensure to maintain the privacy of the users accessing the web services of that organization. The IP addresses, pages accessed and other personal details are anonymized to maintain the commitment of privacy. key characteristics of the dataset are:

- Unique urls: 14
- Unique users: 33
- Total records in the log: 7,324

5.2.2 Dataset D2

For validation purpose, we have taken the data set used for Personalized Web Search Competition (Kaggle, 2011)

The collection includes user sessions with user ids, queries, query phrases, URLs, their domains, URL ranks, and clicks taken from Yandex logs (Yandex, 2015).

To maintain the privacy of the users, information has been completely anonymized. Users' numeric IDs, queries, query phrases, sessions, URLs, and their domains are all disclosed as useless numeric IDs.

key characteristics of the dataset are:

- Unique urls: 703,484,26
- Unique users: 5,736,333
- Total records in the log: 167,413,039

5.3 Data preprocessing

The data which put away in the web server logs are as content file and have missing values and inconsistencies, so we have to preprocess the data before using for analysis purpose. This preprocessing stage will filter out all irrelevant data from analysis.

Sample of log data-

127.0.1.1 - ust [10/Sep/2019:13:55:36 -0700] "GET /abc.htm HTTP/1.0 " 200 2006

127.0.1.1 - ust [10/Sep/2019:13:57:16 -0700] "GET xyz.htm HTTP/1.0 " 230 3428

132.1.0.1 – mak [10/Sep/2019:15:46:56 -0300] "GET uvw.htm HTTP/1.0 " 211 -

127.0.1.1 - ust [11/Sep/2019:03:14:11 -0700] "GET bcd.htm HTTP/1.0 " 249 2326

a. *The first part (127.0.1.1) of the log is the the user's IP address who sent the request to a server.*

b. *The second part after hyphen represent the user id of the person. HTTP authentication determines who is the user.*

c. *The third part ([10/Sep/2019:13:55:36 -0700]) shows the access time using [day/month/year:hour: minute: second zone] format.*

d. *Next part (GET /abc.htm HTTP/1.0) in double quotes, shows the visited page by the client. HTTP 1.0 protocols used for this.*

e. *Next part (200) shows the status code forwarded by the server.*

- *Status code started with 2 --- success*
- *Status code started with 3 --- redirection*
- *Status code started with 4 --- error caused by the client*
- *Status code started with 5 --- error in the server*

f. *The last part (2006) shows us the data size of the content forwarded from server to the client.*

o **Data Cleaning:** Here we remove irrelevant information and entries such like

- entries of failure status messages generated by servers,
- navigational links as redirect and redirection to home page as it is common in many users.

o **User Identification:** Every Unique IP address determines the users.

- ***Session Identification:*** Session is identified with the help of user's navigational behavior and regularly visited pages. The maximum time bound for each session is take as 30 minutes. If a session continues beyond 30 minutes it is considered as another session.

Table 5.1: Sample session details

Users	Session ID	Transitions
U1	S1	P3, P2, P1
	S2	P3, P5, P2, P1, P4
	S3	P4, P5, P2, P1, P5, P4
U2	S4	P3, P4, P5, P2, P3
	S5	P1, P4, P2, P5, P4
U3	S5	P24, P15, P12, P11, P5, P31
	S6	P4, P5, P3, P2, P1, P17
	S7	P2, P5, P4, P8, P19, P23

Table 5.1 represents some samples of user's sessions. For example, user U1 has 3 sessions in the dataset. In session 3 he accesses page 4, page 5, page 2, page 1, page 5 and page 4 respectively.

5.4 User grouping

The users are divided into groups by using k means clustering. The parameters used for clustering purpose are:

- visiting time and date
- pages accessed
- duration

We identified the users by their IP address (assuming that a particular IP is used by only one user). There were total 33 unique users in the dataset we used. After applying k means clustering (for k=4, based on the Grid Search CV) we got the user groups as follows:

Table 5.2: user groups

Users	Group
U3, U7, U8, U22, U28, U29, U33	G1
U4, U2, U14, U16, U17, U20, U26, U34, U32	G2
U1, U6, U10, U15, U24, U25	G3
U5, U9, U11, U12, U13, U18, U19, U21, U23, U27, U30, U31	G4

5.5 Pattern Analysis

Analysis of user's web usage pattern and classify them so that users can be recommended for the services based on their interest (Srivastava et al., 2000).

We are using an Ensemble approach for clustering the users' profiles. First we will apply Association rule mining to generate effective rules for clustering then these rules will be used as an input and we will apply optimization techniques to improve the classification results for classification of user's web usage pattern.

The concept of Association Rule Mining is used to get the association of the most frequent occurring item set (Hipp et al., 2000) for the user's usage pattern as shown in the table 1, where session Id's (S_i) are transactions and pages (P_i) are items.

1. The frequent item sets i.e. pages accessed together in a session having support value more than 0.3 are identified.
2. Association rules are generated and the rules having confidence less than 70% are pruned.

The access patterns having the confidence value above threshold have been selected as most probable usage patterns.

The generated rules are like:

p3∧p4∧p2∧p8	⟶	P5
p3∧p2∧p5	⟶	P4
p1∧p8∧p11∧p13∧p7	⟶	P9
p3∧p2∧p12	⟶	P8

To prune the inefficient rules, the metrics used are support threshold 0.3, confidence threshold 70%. Threshold value for support & confidence are fixed based on experimental results.

5.6 Rule optimization

The rules discovered through APRIORI algorithm (Al-Maolegi & Arkok, 2014) which have been refined using BAT algorithm (X.-S. Yang & He, 2013), a nature inspired optimization technique(Fister Jr et al., 2013).

Three specific rules are used by Yang (X.-S. Yang, 2010) for implementing bats behavior in the algorithm:

- To find the distance all bats use concept of echolocation and by some magical way they differentiate between background hurdles and food.
- Bats look for prey by flying at a random velocity vi at position x_i with a set frequency f_{min}, changing wavelength, and loudness A_0. The wavelength is automatically adjusted depending on the proximity of the target food.
- Although the loudness can change in a variety of ways, we assume that it lies from a large positive value A_0 to a small constant value A_{min}.

For implementation purpose each rule has been handled as a sequence or chromosome of k+1 length, with the 0th position serving as the cut point between the rule's antecedent and consequent. Items are indexed from positions 1 to k, Let the rule X =⇒Y , X =(A₁, A₂, ... , Aⱼ) and Y = (A_{j+1}, A_{j+2}, ..., A_k) is encoded as:

J	I_1	I_2	....	I_j	I_{j+1}	.....	I_n

Let the rule be-

p3∧p4∧p2∧p8 =⇒ p5, will be represented as:

5	0	3	1	2	6	0	0	4	0	0	0	0	0	0

p1∧p8∧p11∧p13∧p7 =⇒ P9, will be represented as:

6	1	0	0	0	0	0	5	2	7	0	3	0	4	0

- **Fitness Function**

we calculated the fitness of each rule based on the rules support and confidence value as proposed by Heraguemi et.al. (Heraguemi et al., 2015) (here a & b are empirical parameters with a=1, b=1).

$$f(R) = \begin{cases} \frac{[a.conf(R)+b.supp(R)]}{a+b} & if\ rule\ accepted \\ -1 & otherwise \end{cases} \qquad \text{Eq. 1}$$

Based on the fitness value, the initial population (set of best rules is obtained from the rules generated through Apriori algorithm).

- **Frequency f_i**

Frequency represents the number of items in a rule which can be changed. Hence the maximum frequency f_{max} can be the total number of page items in the dataset and lowest frequency f_{min} may be 0.

The frequency is updated in iteration k by using the formula:

$$f_{new} = 1 + \mu \cdot f_{max} \qquad \text{Eq.2}$$

Where μ is a random value from the set (0,1)

- **Velocity:**

In our approach velocity represents the position where a change may occur. The velocity parameter is updated in iteration k using the following formula:

$$v_{new} = f_{max} - f_{new} - v_{old} \qquad Eq.3$$

- **Position:**

In our implementation, position are the rules. The position (rules) are updated in iteration k using the steps discussed in (Heraguemi et al., 2014)

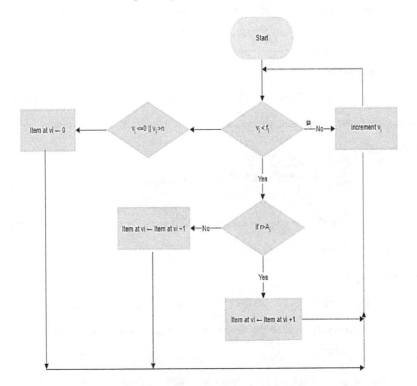

Fig 5.2. Flow chart for implementing virtual BAT motion

Pseudocode for implementing BAT motion:

while (v_i < Frequency f_i) do

if (r > A_i) then # r is random value and A is average loudness

Item at v_i ←− Item at v_i +1   # item at position v_i + 1 position is shifted to position v_i

else

Item at v_i ←− Item at v_i −1   # item at position v_i - 1 position is shifted to position v_i

end if

if (Item at v_i is less or equal to 0 or greater than number of items) then

Item at v_i ←− 0

end if

increment v_i

end while

Steps for generating optimized rules:

i) Initialize the parameters (pulse rate r_i, loudness A_i, population size, no. of iterations).

ii) Update the frequency, velocity of ith bat using equation 2 & 3.

iii) Generate the new position (rule) following the process as per the flowchart.

iv) In each iteration:

    a. If value of rand is greater than r_i (pulse rate)

      i. Generate new rule by changing one item of the rule at a time.

    b. Calculate the fitness values of the new generated rule using equation 1.

    c. If $f(R_{new})$ > $f(R_i)$

      i. Add new rule

      ii. Update pulse rate r_i and loudness A_i

$$r_i^{t+1} = r_i^0[1 - \exp(-\gamma t)] \quad A_i^t = \alpha A_i^{t-1}$$

5.7 Conclusion

In this chapter we have discussed the steps involved in implementation of the proposed system for personalized web page ranking. We have incorporated Apriori algorithm, one of the widely used Association rule mining approach to generate the association rules and then these rules were optimized using BAT algorithm (X.-S. Yang & He, 2013).

All the processes involved were explained with the help of a sample transactional dataset obtained from the dataset D1.

The preprocessing module is used to clean the data and get the session details for our purpose as transactional dataset. In the next phase Apriori algorithm (Al-Maolegi & Arkok, 2014) is used to generate the association rules for providing the next page for navigation based on the association of it with the other parameters used. These rules are stored in the memory pool. The next phase consists of applying BAT algorithm (a nature inspired optimization technique) on the set of rules stored in the memory pool. This phase generates more effective association rules by ignoring the rules having low confidence value below threshold (Kotsiantis & Kanellopoulos, 2006). The more effective rules are then included in the memory pool. This process is repeated by a number of generations.

In this chapter we will discuss the different parameters used for evaluation of the proposed web page ranking system. After that we described our experimental result. At the end we will compare the results of proposed approach with some existing one.

6.1 Evaluation Parameters

The parameters used for validating our proposed system are:

TPR (True Positive Rate): Sensitivity is another name of TPR. The proportion of properly classified point pairs to all point pairs in the same cluster or section is measured by the True Positive Rate (Svetnik et al., 2003).

FPR (False Positive Rate): The intrusion connection of points that were wrongly grouped or categorized is measured by False Positive Rate. (Good result comprises less value of FPR) (Fielding & Bell, 1997).

Accuracy: accuracy is the fraction of correct predictions by the system.

$$A = TP + TN / (TP+TN+FP+FN)$$

Recall: Recall is an evaluation metric that measures how many correct positive predictions were produced out of all possible positive predictions.

$$R = TP/(TP+FN)$$

Precision: Precision refers to the percentage of correctly grouped pairs of points versus all other pairs of points with the same cluster.

$$P = TP/(TP+FP)$$

F-Measure: The harmonic mean of each cluster's precision and recall scores is known as the F-measure. As a result, in all clusters, it attempts to strike a compromise between precision and recall.

$$F\text{-measure} = 2PR/(P+R)$$

6.2 Experimental Results

We have developed an optimized associative classification method for personalized web page ranking using Apriori algorithm i.e. association mining technique and for rule optimization BAT algorithm is used. In this chapter we will show the results of the designed approach and perform a comparative study with state-of-the-art methods.

6.2.1 Results

6.2.1.1 Experiment 1

The proposed system was tested on both the datasets with varying number of iterations. The result of the experiment is shown below:

Table 6.1: Result of the proposed approach with varying number of iterations for D1 & D2

No. of Iterations	Dataset	TPR	FPR	Prec.	Recall	F-measure	Accuracy
50	D1	0.963	0.03	0.969	0.957	0.963	0.89
	D2	0.921	0.028	0.970	0.968	0.969	0.927
100	D1	0.895	0.046	0.951	0.96	0.955	0.92
	D2	0.886	0.06	0.936	0.917	0.926	0.893
150	D1	0.95	0.026	0.973	0.98	0.976	0.88
	D2	0.89	0.048	0.948	0.93	0.939	0.912
Average	D1	0.936	0.034	0.964	0.965	0.965	0.896
	D2	0.899	0.0453	0.951	0.938	0.945	0.912

For dataset D1 we got the highest accuracy of 0.92 with 100 iterations and for D2 we got highest accuracy 0.927 with 50 iterations. The average accuracy of the proposed approach on dataset D1 & D2 is 0.896 and 0.912 respectively.

6.2.1.2 Experiment 2

We have conducted 10 tests for each iteration value on the data set D2 and taken the mean value. The values of different evaluation parameters like precision, recall and F-measure are rounded off to 3 decimal values.

Table 6.2: Result of the proposed approach with varying number of iterations for D2

No. of Iterations	Prec.	Recall	F-measure	Accuracy
50	0.970	0.968	0.969	0.927
100	0.936	0.917	0.926	0.893
150	0.948	0.93	0.939	0.912
400	0.946	0.962	0.954	0.904
700	0.97	0.942	0.951	0.931
1000	0.973	0.949	0.953	0.914
Average	0.957	0.945	0.949	0.9135

In second experiment, we tested the proposed approach on dataset 2 with varying iterations (up to 1000). Although the maximum accuracy we got with 700 iterations, the average accuracy is almost same.

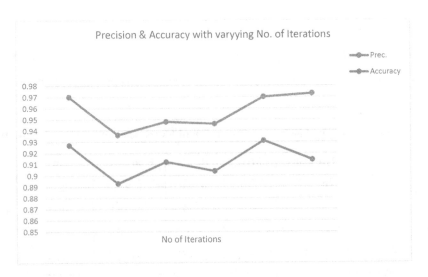

Figure 6.1. Precision & Accuracy of proposed system on D2 dataset

As shown in figure 6.1, although we got maximum precision 0.973 & accuracy value 0.931 for 1000 iterations & 700 iterations respectively, the average accuracy is quite same as in the previous experiment (with iteration 50, 100 & 150).

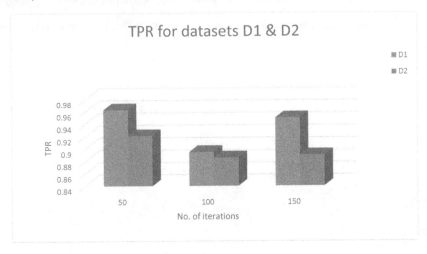

Figure 6.2. TPR value for datasets

Figure 6.2 shows the TPR of the proposed system on the dataset D1 & D2. For both the datasets we got maximum TPR for 50 iterations. For dataset D2 the system provides more consistent TPR compare to the TPR for dataset D1. However, for dataset D1, the system provides maximum TPR value of 0.963 compare to the 0.921 for D2.

Figure 6.3. Precision value for datasets

Figure 6.3 shows the precision of the proposed system on the dataset D1 & D2. For dataset D1, the system provides more precise results with value 0.973 (on 150 iterations) compare to 0.970 (with 50 iterations) for dataset D2.

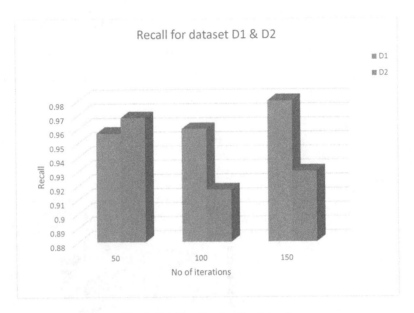

Figure 6.4. Recall value for datasets

Figure 6.4 shows the Recall of the proposed system on the dataset D1 & D2. The proposed system provides maximum recall value 0.980 with 150 iterations on dataset D1, whereas it gives maximum recall value 0.968 on dataset D2 with 50 iterations.

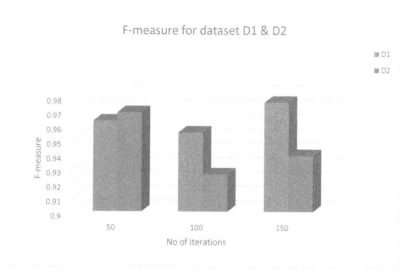

Figure 6.5. F-measure value for datasets

Figure 6.5 shows the F-measure of the proposed system on the dataset D1 & D2. The proposed system provides maximum F-measure value 0.976 with 150 iterations on dataset D1, whereas it provides maximum F-measure value 0.969 on dataset D2 with 50 iterations.

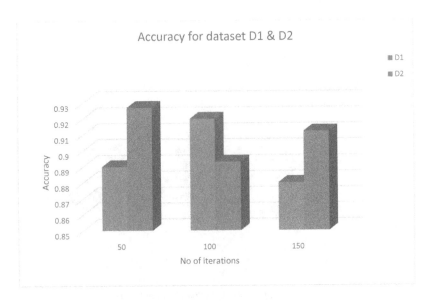

Figure 6.6. Accuracy value for datasets

Figure 6.6 shows the Accuracy of the proposed system on the dataset D1 & D2. The proposed system provides maximum accuracy value 0.920 with 100 iterations on dataset D1, whereas it provides maximum accuracy value 0.927 on dataset D2 with 50 iterations.

The above results show that the proposed system works exceptionally well on dataset D1 compare to dataset D2. However, the performance of the proposed system on dataset D2 is considered to be more realistic as the dataset D1 is a small dataset.

6.3 COMPARATIVE ANALYSIS

Performance of proposed system is validated by means of comparative analysis. In our result we have done two types of comparison:

6.3.1 Comparison to analyze the impact of optimization

We have compared the results of Rules generated without optimization using Apriori algorithm and after the rule optimization using BAT algorithm in terms of total number of rules generated, average support, confidence and accuracy value. Use of BAT algorithm results in the optimized set of rules where the total number of rules get reduced but they have more fitness value and hence the system provides more accuracy. The results are shown below:

Table 6.3 comparison of mined rules without optimization & with optimization

Data-set	No. of Rules generated		Avg. Support		Avg. Confidence		Avg. Accuracy %	
	without optimization	with optimization	without optimization	with optimization	without optimization	with optimization	without optimization	with optimization
D1	173	86	20%	26%	64	52	71	89.6
D2	2886	1849	28	37	78	69	68.3	91.2

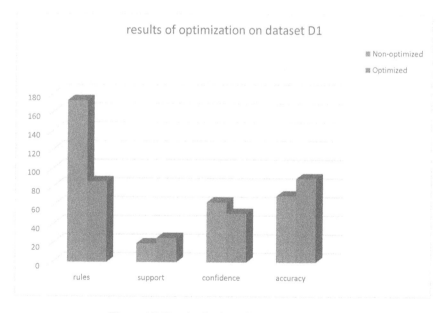

Figure 6.7. Result of rule optimization on D1

6.3.2 Comparison with other works

We have compared the performance of the proposed system with three other state of the art methods and our method performs at par with the current baseline performance outperforms them in terms of precision.

Table 6.4 comparison of proposed method with others

Approach	TPR	FPR	Prec.	Recall	F-measure	Accuracy
(Al-Asdi & Obaid, 2016)	0.935	0.031	0.938	0.935	0.952	--
(Chawla, 2016)	--	--	0.77	--	--	--
(Malhotra & Rishi, 2018)	--	--	0.906	0.935	0.925	90.74
Proposed Approach	0.899	0.0453	0.951	0.938	0.945	91.2

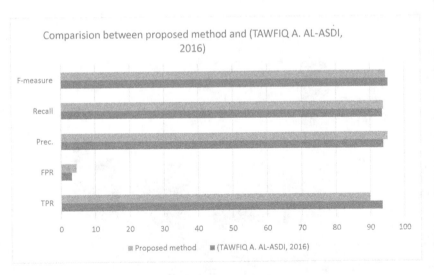

Figure 6.8 comparison of proposed method with ref. (Al-Asdi & Obaid, 2016)

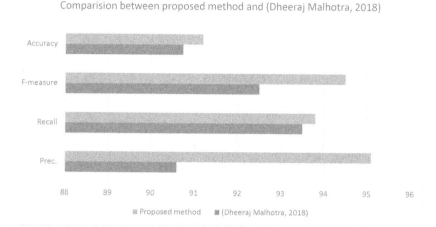

Figure 6.9 comparison of proposed method with ref. (Malhotra & Rishi, 2018)

6.4 Conclusion

In this chapter we have discussed the results of the proposed optimized system based on association rule mining approach and BAT algorithm for personalized web page ranking.

The proposed approach was tested on 2 different datasets. We have validated the performance evaluation of the defined proposed approach by different number of iterations. We have also presented the comparative result between simple association rule mining (without optimization) and after getting optimized rules using BAT algorithm. The results of the proposed system were also compared with some of the state-of-the-art methods.

In order to provide effective personalized web page ranking based on user's web usage behavior, this work proposed a novel approach based on optimized association rule mining. The approach was applied to two different datasets for training and testing purpose. The comparative result indicates that the proposed approach shows improved accuracy by optimizing the rule set generated by association rules.

7.1 Conclusion

Web page ranking assists us to navigate highly ranked pages to the user that are relevant to the query. So it is an important task to rank the pages on personalized manner. A series of metrics have been defined to rank the web pages as per their quality.

With the help of web usage analysis, we can effectively improve the ranking of the web pages according to the user's requirement (Langville & Meyer, 2011; Matthijs & Radlinski, 2011).

The objective of the proposed research work was to provide an efficient technique for personalized web page ranking of search engine based on web usage analysis.

The web page personalization based on web mining technique has two major phases, offline and online. The objective of the offline phase is to model user's navigation pattern using the history, web log data. This model is used in online phase to predict a user navigation pattern and give recommendations to them based on prediction.

We have collected implicit user information. Implicit data is the past user activity data which automatically stored in web server logs without their knowledge.

In our research work, we have designed and implemented a novel system for personalized web page ranking based on web usage analysis. This research proposal gives inspiring results in compare to some other state of the art methods (Jagan & Rajagopalan, 2015).

The proposed system has been implemented in two phases, first we have used Apriori algorithm (Al-Maolegi & Arkok, 2014), to generate the initial population of rules. After that we have used BAT algorithm to get the set of most efficient rules to provide the most probable next page for navigation (Yılmaz & Küçüksille, 2015).

We have tested the system by varying number of iterations from 50 to 1000. The proposed system gives maximum accuracy of 93% after 700 iterations (for dataset D2) and overall average accuracy of 91.2%.

Following points can be concluded based on the work done:

- For efficient response to the user query, the ranking of web pages retrieved by the search engine is very critical.
- We can predict the interest of the user based on his web usage; this can be used to improve the ranking of the web pages retrieved.
- The kNN mechanism of standard collaborative filtering for personalization involves in real time evaluation of user records both current and historical. But the major drawback of this mechanism is as the number of users increase this will become impractical, ie. kNN cannot deal with large volume of data.
- Association mining had proved that it can easily predict user browsing behavior for web personalized recommendation. Even though it predicts the pattern but because of the low coordinating rate of the subsequent tenets and different in scanning conduct of the user the application of it for predicting future pattern is low.

- Converting the log data into useful set of records for the analysis purpose is a time taking and complex process.
- Getting dataset was not easy. The datasets available in public domain are having too old data (19's or early 2000). Organizations were not ready to share their log data.

The important contributions of this work:

- We have proposed and implemented a novel approach which makes use of Association Mining and one of the latest metaheuristic optimization techniques that takes the benefits of echolocation behavior of bats to predict the best ranking of webpages.
- We have implemented and tested the proposed system on two different datasets.
- Although some of the researchers have implemented association mining rule for ranking purpose, but the result shows that the optimization of rule set produced much improved results.
- We have performed a comparative study of the system without optimization and with optimization on the parameters like number of rules generated in the rule set, average support value, confidence value and accuracy.
- Proposed approach gives the average accuracy of 91.2%, precision value 95.1% and recall 93.8% which is much encouraging result in comparison of other state of the art techniques.
- We have performed a series of comparison and analyze the proposed approach with some other existing approaches and the results are encouraging.

7.2 Future Work

The implementation of BAT algorithm to optimize the generated rule set has shown positive impact in the system performance as shown in the table 6.3. However, there are certain aspects which we are looking to work in future.

There are different parameters in BAT algorithm which can be optimized for more efficient results. We are planning to test our system with multiple pulse emissions in different directions. Controlling and varying the parameters like loudness and pulse rate can also be worth exploring in the future.

The results of the proposed system also encourage us to incorporate the proposed concept in other real-life problems

Introduction

With the advent of high-speed internet and the rise in smartphone internet-users has resulted in a massive surge of internet data on the World Wide Web. As there is no centralized monitoring of data to be stored, indexed, and retrieved out there on the web, Search Engines face a challenging task of retrieving queried information from the Web, not only in a timely manner, but also to the exact and close accuracy of users' interest and their intent. As a result of the exponential growth in digital data on the World Wide Web, Search Engines must be clever and capable enough to obtain the searched information serving & befitting the needs and preferences of internet users. For this purpose, ranking web pages emerges as viable solution to cater this challenge and becomes a heroic task by helping users in finding highly rated web-pages that are believed to be the most relevant to their intended search and purpose. The solution thus achieved is referred as "Personalized web search using page ranking approach".

In order to provide effective personalized web page ranking based on user's web usage behavior, this work proposes a novel approach based on optimized association rule mining. The approach was applied to two different datasets for training and testing purpose. The comparative result indicates that the proposed approach shows improved accuracy by optimizing the rule set generated by association rules.

Conclusion

Web page ranking assists us to navigate highly ranked pages to the user that are relevant to the query. So, it is an important task to rank the pages on personalized manner. A series of metrics have been defined to rank the web pages as per their quality.

With the help of web usage analysis, we can effectively improve the ranking of the web pages according to the user's requirement (Langville & Meyer, 2011; Matthijs & Radlinski, 2011).

The objective of the proposed research work was to provide an efficient technique for personalized web page ranking of search engine based on web usage analysis.

The web page personalization based on web mining technique has two major phases, offline and online. The objective of the offline phase is to model user's navigation pattern using the history, web log data. This model is used in online phase to predict a user navigation pattern and give recommendations to them based on prediction.

We have collected implicit user information. Implicit data is the past user activity data which automatically stored in web server logs without their knowledge.

In our research work, we have designed and implemented a novel system for personalized web page ranking based on web usage analysis. This research proposal gives inspiring results in compare to some other state of the art methods (Jagan & Rajagopalan, 2015).

The proposed system has been implemented in two phases, first we have used Apriori algorithm (Al-Maolegi & Arkok, 2014), to generate the initial population of rules. After that we have used BAT algorithm to get the set of most efficient rules to provide the most probable next page for navigation (Yılmaz & Küçüksille, 2015).

We have tested the system by varying number of iterations from 50 to 1000. The proposed system gives maximum accuracy of 93% after 700 iterations (for dataset D2) and overall average accuracy of 91.2%.

Following points can be concluded based on the work done:

- For efficient response to the user query, the ranking of web pages retrieved by the search engine is very critical.
- We can predict the interest of the user based on his web usage; this can be used to improve the ranking of the web pages retrieved.
- The kNN mechanism of standard collaborative filtering for personalization involves in real time evaluation of user records both current and historical. But the major drawback of this mechanism is as the number of users increase this will become impractical, ie. kNN cannot deal with large volume of data.
- Association mining had proved that it can easily predict user browsing behavior for web personalized recommendation. Even though it predicts the pattern but because of the low coordinating rate of the subsequent tenets and different in scanning conduct of the user the application of it for predicting future pattern is low.
- Converting the log data into useful set of records for the analysis purpose is a time taking and complex process.
- Getting dataset was not easy. The datasets available in public domain are having too old data (19's or early 2000). Organizations were not ready to share their log data.

The important contributions of this work:

- We have proposed and implemented a novel approach which makes use of Association Mining and one of the latest metaheuristic optimization techniques that takes the benefits of echolocation behavior of bats to predict the best ranking of webpages.
- We have implemented and tested the proposed system on two different datasets.

- Although some of the researchers have implemented association mining rule for ranking purpose, but the result shows that the optimization of rule set produced much improved results.
- We have performed a comparative study of the system without optimization and with optimization on the parameters like number of rules generated in the rule set, average support value, confidence value and accuracy.
- Proposed approach gives the average accuracy of 91.2%, precision value 95.1% and recall 93.8% which is much encouraging result in comparison of other state of the art techniques.
- We have performed a series of comparison and analyze the proposed approach with some other existing approaches and the results are encouraging.

Future Work

The implementation of BAT algorithm to optimize the generated rule set has shown positive impact in the system performance as shown in the table 6.3. However, there are certain aspects which we are looking to work in future.

There are different parameters in BAT algorithm which can be optimized for more efficient results. We are planning to test our system with multiple pulse emissions in different directions. Controlling and varying the parameters like loudness and pulse rate can also be worth exploring in the future.

The results of the proposed system also encourage us to incorporate the proposed concept in other real-life problems.

Mohammad Suaib

CPSIA information can be obtained
at www.ICGtesting.com
Printed in the USA
LVHW081317141222
735075LV00026B/1439